The Sacred Dance

New Possibilities For Later Life

Roger Douglas

Table of Contents

To C.B. whose interests and encouragement made this book possible. Thank you for helping me to believe in myself.

Preface

Roger Douglas is a friend and colleague—an elder that I respect and admire—who, in this significant book on growing older, brings to us some answers to a critical question that he raises: "How do older people find purpose and meaning in their life in a culture where they no longer seem to serve any purpose?" Correctly he identifies the reality that, in America, there are two problems with aging: "The attitude of society toward the old, and the attitude of the old to being old." It is this latter problem that he provides the most direction in this book.

Roger has lived the journey—the pilgrimage—into the older years, first writing a book on retirement, *The Pilgrim Season,* and now writing a wise and important book on what it means to be old when we are old. He has learned from his own experience, which he readily shares, and from others who he has taught and counseled, that this is not an easy journey. It is difficult. He outlines this in his first chapter on "What is Old?" However, he asks us to consider traveling new pathways that can give us that sense of meaning and purpose that we all want as we grow older.

The heart of the book lies in what Roger has called, *Pathway Narratives*, the story lines, the paths by which we move on our journey through life, the stories that connect our identity with our personal experience. The narrative is our inner instruction, our pathway on how to live the good life at this age. He writes:

"I am convinced that there are several paths that people take as we go into the afternoon of life. The choices we make, the decisions we undertake, the transitions we face, and the ways we react to what people call normal aging problems, are not dependent upon chronological age, but more dependent upon the narratives we have about ourselves and the way we deal with what we call reality."

He continues by suggesting that dealing with the struggle between the "hardening of the narrative and changing the narrative" is the critical message of the book. This, he rightly concludes, arises out of our transitions when we move from one stable place (an old narrative) to a new place (a new narrative). It is, as he writes, a *Metanoia,* a turning around, an inner reorientation.

The five *Pathway Narratives*, offer us a way to help us figure out where we are in the aging process. Roger recognizes that these five pathways are not exclusive and that each of us may invent our own and that there is no one way to maturity. What the pathways do is provide us with a beginning for conversations that are so very critical in finding meaning and purpose as we grow older.

I have enjoyed this book, and I have struggled with it because it has challenged me. It has engaged me. I have appreciated Roger's use of significant writers who have written on this topic and his exploration into our faith experience. Most of all, I resonated with his message of *The Sacred Dance*:

Do not be mindful with what is beyond your control. Your dance may not be the same as your neighbors. Don't be concerned over the right steps. Just remember nobody looks natural when they dance. When you cease asking for guarantees and stop demanding certainty, your feet will take care of themselves. Dancing the sacred dance is the clue to maturity in the second half of life.

The Rev. Dr. Frank R. Williams
Social Services Director
Casa de la Luz Hospice
Tucson, Arizona

Introduction

"No more deadlines. No more coats and ties. No more need to early rise."

Retirement seems to be a hot topic in the American consciousness.

Experts are offering advice and counsel for persons in their post-retirement years, and how-to books flourish on ways to plan ahead successfully. In order to succeed under the current rash of advice, you need to know exactly when to retire and when to die. Getting the retirement income right means that you have to have an adequate handle on income flow, inflation, medical care, assisted living and other factors that will have impact on the later years. A whole new industry has evolved to help people transition to the second half of life.

Several factors have caused us to change our thinking on aging. Seventy-five years ago, it made sense for the labor leader Walter Reuther to say, "Retirement is the time in a persons life when one is too old to work and too young to die." No longer can we treat this period as a short unimportant time. Living to age ninety is no longer unusual. Medicine and science have not only increased our lives, they have also enabled us to live with better health and greater mobility. Transportation has improved, which has given us the freedom of not necessarily having to live close to younger family members. As birth rates decline, the elderly gain a larger percentage of the overall population. The fact of the matter is that we are an aging society. Medical science may have given us a blessing, however we often act as if it were a disease. More money and time are spent on concealing the signs of old age than in dealing with cancer or heart disease.

Most writers have continued to speak of aging as the shift from an active to a passive time of life. In the 1960's Del Webb tried to remedy the sense of loss that hung over retirement by creating a special community for those over 55 in Sun City, Arizona. This expressed Webb's vision that after a life of work, a person should be rewarded with a life of leisure

As the new century began, some writers questioned Webb's vision of retirement. They began to see the later stages of life to be more than endless golf and cocktail parties.

Redirection rather than retirement began to be explored. The question was raised: How do older people find purpose and meaning in their life in a culture where they no longer seem to serve any purpose? Aging in America basically presents us with twin problems--he attitude of society toward the old, and the attitude of the old to being old.

All of these modern writers owe a debt of gratitude to two men who made us aware that the post-retirement years needed a new focus. There was a way to find meaning in the years after sixty.

Carl Jung wrote: "A human being would certainly not grow to be 70 or 80 years old if this longevity had no meaning for the species to which he belongs. The afternoon of human life must also have a significance of its own and cannot be merely a pitiful appendage of life's morning. Whoever carries over into the afternoon the law of the morning--that is, the aims of nature--must pay for so doing with damage to his soul just as surely as a growing youth who tries to salvage his childish egoism must pay for this mistake with a social failure."

After Jung came the developmental psychologist Erik Erikson whose eight stages of life laid the foundation for modern studies. He wrote of aging moving from trust, to autonomy, to initiative, to industry, to identity, to intimacy, to generativity, and finally to ego integrity. Erickson was the lone voice for many years who viewed the later years as a process rather than a destination. It's interesting to note that as he and his wife Joan moved into their 80's, they expanded their theory of aging to include a ninth stage. They called this "the life cycle completed." They described it as the stage where one was able to ward off the despair that gradual physical disintegration produced by connecting it to the sense of completeness. The great contribution of the Ericksons was that aging was seen as a dynamic process, and that a person shifted from one stage to another not by adding years, but rather by doing the work and avoiding things like stagnation and despair. If one went through these stages successfully, this would lead one into a deeper state of wisdom. Failure resulted in bitterness, regret, and despair. The focus on process and maturity put the Eriksons far ahead of those who simply saw aging as an enemy that needed to be denied or defeated.

As a priest for more than fifty years, and having worked closely with many who are in the process of major life changes, I bring a somewhat different perspective to the issue of aging. I have observed that many of the assumptions based on age categories are not applicable. Some people die at sixty but are not buried until they are eighty. Oliver Wendell Holmes once wrote:

"Some people you know as they approach 70 begin to read the Bible and prepare to die, others prepare to live till they are 90. Now if the ones who prepare to live to 90 die at 70, they won't know the difference. But if the ones who prepare to die at 70 live until they are 90, then the last 20 years would be hell." The passage of years is a poor indicator of where we stand in the life cycle. The problem is that there are not many valid teachers to guide us through these difficult years.

Some fifteen years ago I wrote a book on retirement. At that time I was newly retired and I attempted to find new meanings to this stage of life. Instead of seeing the afternoon of life as a single entity, I put forth the idea that the journey into retirement was a pilgrimage and tried to show how this gave meaning to the whole aging process. A pilgrim in the old sense of the word was a traveler passing through this world. Now, having taught several classes for older citizens, and with new insight into the changes that elderly people go through, I am convinced that there are several paths that people take as we move into the afternoon of life. The choices we make, the decisions we undertake, the transitions we face, and the ways we react to what people call normal aging problems are not dependent upon chronological age, but more dependent upon the narratives we have about ourselves and the way we deal with what we call reality.

A key component in determining one's narrative is not as many people think, a matter of age, health, or past experiences in the first half of life. The important factors were values, faith, self-understanding and assumptions we made of the future.

As a child, I can recall being told that the only two things one can count upon were death and taxes. Now there is a third part to that saying. Change is the one other constant factor in a very chaotic world. The way we face change, the way we take risks, the way we leave our comfort zones are dependent on our narratives.

Too often we have viewed the afternoon of life as a sort of plateau with a single narrative that lasts until death draws it all to a close. My observations have been that this period in the life cycle is a dynamic, changing time. As we age we take steps away from narratives that we have inherited from our families and our culture. To mature, as we age, we have to be able to view our narratives with a somewhat jaundiced eye, and we have to be able to move on to other narratives.

All of us are getting older, and as we age we develop tactics to handle change. One such tactic is to evolve a philosophy that helps us understand the physical and emotional changes. A negative tactic is to play the blame game. Some of us simply look around for enemies to blame for our condition--society, our boss, the culture, the government. Some, after a certain point in their lives, just give up, stop dreaming, stop hoping. After retirement they view life as a process of going to seed, breaking down, and facing deteriorating health. And some who believed the fairy tale formula, "And they lived happily ever after," have found reality as something else. To those, the second half of life is, at best, boring and at worst frightening. They were masters of the universe yesterday and find themselves outcasts today. Much needless suffering has come about because we have not taken this stage of life seriously enough nor developed a mature understanding of aging. They might have developed a financial plan to safeguard their monies, but rarely do they have a spiritual plan to carry them through the later years of their life.

Still there are a few who find the afternoon of life exciting, life affirming, and an opportunity to change the story of their life. For these people, the afternoon of life is about an inner journey, a challenge to walk through unchartered waters, an opportunity to mature spiritually, and an occasion to renew a relationship to God. As the poet Robert Browning said: "Grow old along with me, the best is yet to be."

Back in 1931, Carl Jung wrote that the afternoon of life is radically different from the morning and has to be managed in a different fashion. "But where," he asked, "are the universities to prepare us for this stage of our lives."

A good deal of time has elapsed since Jung wrote those words, and we still do not have a university for seniors. A university where wise persons could teach potentially wise persons, where the purpose of learning is not for a career, but learning for learning sake. The goal of the university would not be to keep old persons busy or entertained, but rather to remind them that every moment is an opportunity to mature.

The reason this book was written is to stimulate one's imagination in such a way that you discover the second half of life to be a period of excitement, renewal and discovery. Just as I have observed that most sermons are really directed at the preacher, so too are most books written to the author. Initially, I began to write about change and the many ways we respond to the rapidly changing world. But, the deeper I delved into change, the more I found much depended upon the individual's inner narrative. Two people are confronted with the same changing circumstance but they react in vastly different ways. As I began writing about change, I set out to find why this was so. The more I researched, the more I found a correlation between change and the inner dialogue which I am calling *an individual's narrative.* If you're like me, you are a slow learner and need someone to raise the essential questions about this stage of life. Often times it is the poets, not the scientists nor the academics, who would have us ponder about this thing called aging.

> *Doesn't everything die at last, and too soon?*
>
> *Tell me, what is it you plan to do*
>
> *with your one wild and precious life?"*
>
> Lines from *The Summer Day* by Mary Oliver, *House of Light*, Beacon Press

Chapter One: Who is Old?

Society has many subtle and not so subtle ways of informing us that we are in the stage of life called old.

Not long ago I was riding on a crowded bus that meandered around a busy airport. All the seats were occupied. As I moved toward the rear a young man rose and said: "Here Sir, take my seat." My wife went to the doctor for our annual check up. She began describing some minor problems. The doctor replied; "Well at your age, you can expect...." What is the meaning of old? When are we seen as elderly? How do we recognize that we have passed from the morning to the afternoon of life? Does it have to do with our chronological age? Is 60 somehow the dividing line or is it three score years and ten? Do we suddenly get a message that is addressed, dear Senior? The Association of Retired Persons uses age 55 as the beginning of the second half of life. At that age you are welcome to join a club that grants certain privileges and discounts. Possibly it is the government that decides we are old when Medicare's eligibility starts at age 65. Is that the beginning of the 2nd half of life? Recently I came across a list of things that will let you know if you are *old*. The list runs from the ridiculous to the serious. From, "when your back goes out more than you do, or when you get winded playing checkers." Then the announcement is more serious when "You've gotten to the top of the ladder and found its against the wrong wall." What then is it that defines what we have sometimes euphemistically called the golden years? T.S. Eliot once wrote; "I don't believe one grows older. I think that what happens early on in life is that at a certain age one stands still and stagnates." If his analysis is correct, maybe we ought to call the years after 60, the years of boredom and monotony. The French essayist Montaigne also wrote a definition of old age. It was "a decay of the powers...a powerful disease that steals upon us naturally and imperceptibly."

Most early writers have pictured old age as too frightening to contemplate.

As early as 1905, William Osler, an influential doctor and scientist, identified the biological age that determined life's' cycle. After youth, according to Osler, we have before us creative years that fall between the ages of 25 and 40. After 40, we live through the non-creative years in which little can be expected. A rather dire prediction!

The early literature on aging simply treated old age

as coming upon us when we ceased to be productive. We then could seek wisdom rather then accomplishments. This was so because, in our American culture, everything seems to cease at middle age. We find it particularly hard in a youth culture where we are expected to accumulate power, wealth, and control. Then suddenly we find that these areas no longer have meaning. Privileges and relationships are changed. We lose our status and we feel we have outlasted our usefulness, perhaps other than for baby-sitting chores. It is at this stage we introduce terms such as *old*. We seem to forget that this stage of life can go on for thirty years or more.

As a pastor, I have watched people become old over night. It had nothing to do with age or circumstances. There was something in their inner journey that signaled the time had come to be old. As I set out to identify these inner signals, I discovered that there was a narrative in most peoples lives that explained their inner reality.

Thomas Cole in *The journey of life, A Cultural History of Aging in America* examines how the West's ancient understanding of aging has been upended by a scientific world view. In previous centuries, growing old was a spiritual mystery in the eternal order of life. Now Cole points out, it is a scientific problem to be managed or solved. We talk of genes and maintaining life's balance rather than seeing it all as a gift from God.

More specifically, many of the present day gerontologists focus on chronological age ranges. Specifically some gerontologists have divided age ranges in about ten year segments. They have attempted to divide this period of life into three distinct stages. They then refer to physical characteristics as they appear in the young old, middle old, and old old. Chronologically they think of aging by these three distinct periods, 60-74, 75-84, 85-until death. These are convenient markers for understanding physical deterioration, but they say little about the inner journey. They also say little about our human search for meaning and for maturity as we add years to our life.

The professional gerontologists who catalog the boundaries for understanding physical deterioration of the human body may provide a helpful analysis of what generally happens to people as they age, but there are so many exceptions that it hardly seems an adequate way to observe the aging process.

So when are we old and when does it begin? The real problem is that the vocabulary that we commonly use for the first half of life differs immeasurably from our descriptions of the afternoon of life.

In the first half of life we measured our lives in categories that fell under the headings of productivity or achievements or our identity. In the second of life we use words like meaning, inner journey, and beginning again to describe some of the issues we face. In the morning of life we are interested in growth, power, a family, a nest egg, a reputation. In the evening of life we are interested in maturing, coming to terms with life and learning to say hello and good-bye to people and things.

One major obstacle in our understanding of old age is our theory of humanity. Basically there are two prevalent understandings. One is the mechanistic view where life is defined exclusively in terms of function and activity. Like a car, it emerges from the morning of life at its finest. Then at a certain point these functions begin to deteriorate. This is when we might say the downward spiral begins. The machine worked well in our youth and middle years, but now the repair bills mount, the joints creak, and our eyes and ears are wearing out. Like a car we are ready for a trade or for the junk heap. It is easy to understand that, with this theory, we rapidly see ourselves as elderly, or vintage or just plain worn out as we age. This mechanistic view comes from a culture that views productivity over community, answers over questions, growth over maturity. Isak Dinesen wrote:

"Life is a process for turning fat playful puppies into mangy old dogs. We know what we have to do with an old dog once it's past its prime. When it can't see, and can't hear, and can't look after its own interests, we put it to sleep."

Sometimes we stumble upon a different view of humanity. It is more Eastern in its orientation. It is more of a developmental view and more akin to ripening, and like old wine, gets better with age. Aging is not a downhill slope. The developmental view is a different understanding of the term old. It is where we describe our identity changes and take on different tasks. Old age is a process of moving into a new stage of life's journey. The Hindu concept of life divides aging in three stages. The first stage is the student, where learning is the key. The second stage the householder, where family, job, and achievement are the principle concerns. The last stage is called going into the forest, where assimilation and solitude, reflection and integration are the main undertakings. Doctor Percy Gresham described this stage for Americans as, "It's where you can mount up on the wings of eagles, learn to set priorities, stay well, and become spiritually mature."

Old age, what is it? You can't avoid it if you continue living. Is it really a state of mind rather than a chronological age? Can you avoid it by merely slowing down instead of stopping whatever has been your career? Does it have more to do with maturity than growth? Is it more about your place in the world and your assumptions about reality than whether you physically can function as well as you used to? To deny the afternoon of life is to never fully grow up. To face the many changes over time is the beginning of maturity.

As Kirk, a member of a group on aging put it: "The world I thought would be waiting when I turned sixty simply wasn't there. And it still isn't. The country I thought would be present when I had my last birthday simply wasn't there when I blew out the candles this year. The system I counted on, the institutions I depended upon, the leaders I trusted simply aren't there anymore. As I've aged, I have begun to wonder if they ever were there."

Betty Friedan, one of the leaders of the feminist revolution in the sixties, began the preface of her last book with these words: "When my friends threw a surprise party on my 60th birthday, I could have killed them all. Their toasts seemed hostile...pushing me out of the race...I was depressed for weeks after that birthday party, felt removed from them all."

The transition from the morning to the afternoon

of life is really a mystery. We often respond to mystery with anger and denial. The more we reflect on becoming or being old, the harder it is to think only about physical aging. Something deeper is happening. Life invites us to let go of a particular kind of self image and the ways we had developed to cope in the morning of life. Barbara Fried writes that "death is the frame for the picture of the second half of life." But regardless of the frame, aging in the later half of life finds us coping with feelings and questions that have remained dormant for years.

At special moments like birthdays, those feeling tend to emerge. We find ourselves questioning the advancing years. Is it really an advance or is it a retreat? We sometimes say; "Oh I never celebrate my Birthday." Or, "We feel the same as we did five years ago. Why have a party?" These are just some of the ways that we avoid facing the basic question: What is happening as I age? What is going on inside of me as another year passes? Am I growing or shrinking as a spiritual person?

When I am an old woman, I shall wear purple

With a red hat which doesn't go, and doesn't suit me.

And I shall spend my pension on brandy and summer gloves

And satin sandals, and say we've no money for butter.

I shall sit down on the pavement when I'm tired

And gobble up samples in shops and press alarm bells

And run my stick along the public railings

And make up for the sobriety of my youth.

I shall go out in my slippers in the rain

And pick the flowers in other people's gardens

And learn to spit.

An excerpt from a poem called *Warning* by Jenny Joseph, Papier-Mache Press

Chapter Two: Narratives

What is a narrative? Let me start our thinking about narratives in the second half of life by a definition of terms. An aging narrative is a story line that connects one's identity with a person's experience. It is the path by which we move on our journey through life. Narratives helps us set boundaries, establish beliefs, and clarify the rules of the game. We all possess a narrative or are a narrative that affirms our values. It says a great deal about our assumptions and the myths we hold. Narratives are pathways to understanding who we are and where we are going. Narratives are the pathways that emerge as we experience the ups and downs of life. Admittedly this use of narratives is different from the common use of the word narrative.

While our life cycle can be seen as a record of events, our narrative solidifies the events into a story line. It is a valuable clue as to how we react to health issues, financial matters, relationship concerns. It is, in general, how we face the aging process. Each of us creates a kind of working hypothesis or inner narrative which tells us what we believe and where we are headed.

The trouble is that we don't often revise these inner narratives. We keep fitting new experiences into old slots.

We have often said "I see, then I believe." We usually believe and then we see. Belief here refers to one's inner narrative. Narratives act as psychological filters by which we see the world. What may be perfectly visible to one person may be invisible to another, because one narrative doesn't fit the other. Einstein said: "We see what our theories permit us to see." It's not true that we have certain experiences and then we go shopping around for a theory that makes sense of these experiences. What happens is that we have certain expectations or beliefs, and these beliefs or theories enable us to see. This is the key to what ladder we climb as we age as well as the story we tell about our actions. These stories are carried in our minds and are part of our subconscious. They are important because they help us locate our comfort zones and describe what is true for us at the time.

Another reason why narratives are important was supplied by William James. At a meeting of the American Psychological Association he was asked what was the most important finding of the first half of the century as far as the human mind. His reply was: "People by and large become what they think of themselves." The narratives we have are the storylines that explain what we think of ourselves. They are not necessarily perfect. Even the most cherished narratives may be lacking from our present perspective. At twenty we might have seen ourselves as immortal, but by the time we reach 80 we know that death enters the picture. It is not that the narrative at any age is wrong; it is just incomplete.

One example of a narrative that is popular in the first half of life is the Horatio Alger story. This tells us that we can pull ourselves up by our boot straps. By trying harder we can move from rags to riches. The playing field is level and we have just as good a chance to succeed as the next person. Whether this is true or not is inconsequential. If this is a part of our narrative, then we will believe the boundaries in life are open, and the path is one that believes that hard work will be rewarded.

There are three functions to a narrative. First a narrative is to waken and maintain in the individual a sense of order and participation in the mystery of this inscrutable universe. It gives a definite clue as to how to behave inside the boundaries of this new condition called aging. The narrative is your inner instruction, your pathway on how to live the good life at this age.

A second function of a narrative validates and maintains whatever moral system and manner of life to which one subscribes. It is often shaped by religious training. It helps in understanding why we were created and for what purpose. Since, by definition, narratives are ongoing and temporary insights into how we see reality, we can then live with the evolving nature of truth and beliefs.

The third function is the pedagogical one. This tends to keep individuals living in harmony through the passages of human life. We learn through our narratives how to be a winner on our journey. Of course the term winner is different in the second half of life. We might say that we live in a perpetual confrontation between external success, being a winner in the first half of life, and the internal values of maturity in the second half.

In *The Pilgrim Season,* my previous book on aging, there was a chapter called, "The Bible never talks about retirement." No matter how hard I had searched, I never could locate any Scripture dealing with people who had retired or stopped working, or received a pension, or had taken up some leisure activity. It surely never occurred to a St. Paul to think, "I'm tired of traveling and controversy. I think it's time for me to retire?" Despite this seeming deficiency, the Bible is very clear about the different narratives in the second half of life.

Take the story of Abraham from the book of

Genesis. This really can be seen as an extended metaphor for the aging process. Whether there was a person called Abram, whether he was married or had children doesn't matter. The story is really about changing one's narrative as we grow older.

We read in Genesis, that Abram lived in a place called Harem. In the first half of his life he has done well, achieved a modicum of success, climbed the ladder called *the Good life.* At 75 something happens. He enters the afternoon of life. He faces one of those transition moments. Suddenly, the narrative changes and he is on a new and different path. The ladder he was climbing in the first half of life is now against a different wall. The way the Bible tells it, God speaks and asks that he leave Harem and go out to the unknown. I believe this is a metaphor for choosing a new narrative in the 2nd half of life. The new narrative is about loss, it's about leaving one's comfort zone, and it's about taking up one's calling. In the course of this new pathway, Abram's identity changes, and at the end of the journey he assumes the name Abraham, the father of a new tribe of people. This signals an entirely different narrative than he had for the first 75 years. Back in Harem, his narrative had to do with being a merchant and a family man who is moderately successful, as success was measured by the people of his day.

We think that most change happens in the first half of life. This is not necessarily so. The story in Genesis is an important correction to what is commonly held. People can and do significantly change in the afternoon of life. Scripture also reminds us that in the vintage years we often begin to express a true sense of vocation. Simeon, Joseph of Aramethea, Moses, Elijah, are just a few of the Biblical figures who discovered a holy path in the afternoon of life. Did you ever realize that St. Paul was about 60 when he began his extensive ministry?

Aging is an opportunity to break with social and parental conditioning that has made us assume certain narratives. Take the story line from an earlier narrative, "Father knows best." The narrative is about the assumption that what our parents taught us is the right way to do things. As we age, we might take on a different narrative with the story line "I can make my own decisions." The narrative then is about one's self-identity and the ability to make one's own mistakes. The narrative is what gives us an understanding of maturity and tells us how we might face the changing world. Narratives are important clues to finding one's own voice.

Many who have struggled to develop a narrative that fits their circumstances in the first half of life feel particularly anxious when they are faced with changing the narrative in the second half of life. They will say, "What you mean is that the ladder I have been steadily climbing is against the wrong wall?" Or as a 70 year old friend recently wrote: "Now that I've gotten my act together, the play has been changed." A response to her might be, now that you are in the elderly category, "You're no longer in Kansas, Dorothy."

There are, of course, books that give us roadmaps to the later years. suggesting what we ought to be doing. They are misleading. The whole concept that one can choose a pattern as one enters the afternoon of life, and that one can predict the direction of life's changes is questionable. The truth is that there are several factors that influence us in choosing a narrative. Some of these factors are: past experiences, maturity levels, and whatever we call our faith. All combine to help us choose an appropriate narrative and contribute to any changes we might make to the old one. The business of faith, or lack thereof, is probably the most important variable in choosing our narratives.

In a collection of letters Flannery O'Connor reflected on the place of faith. She had received a letter from a friend complaining that a women they both knew had gotten involved in religion after her husband had died. Her friend wrote: "I am always a bit troubled when people regard faith as chiefly a compensation."

But O'Connor wrote back: "Maybe so. On the other hand, some kind of loss is usually necessary to turn the mind toward faith. If you're satisfied with what you've got, you're hardly looking for anything better."

Why do we include faith as a necessary component to an aging narrative? Carl Jung gives us a clue to this question. He writes: "Among all my patients in the second half of life, there has not been one whose problem in the last resort was not that of finding a religious outlook on life."

In the middle ages a great deal was made over the art of dying (ars moriendi). The main purposes of faith has always been to help one die well. Now we don't want to die at all. We want to have time to get our life in order, to heal what needs healing, and to make sense out of our days here on earth. This is where one's faith becomes operative in the 21st century. Our faith certainly is a prime factor in making a choice between narratives.

Choose we must, particularly as we find the narratives of the past to be inadequate to the challenges as we face the aging process. Thomas Cole in "The Journey of life" reminds us that aging is a season in search of its purpose. The narrative is how we personalize the search. It's the story we carry in our heads about ourselves which gives us the pathway we choose as we climb the ladder called aging.

> *And if you are lost*
>
> *enough to find yourself*
>
> *By now pull in your ladder*
>
> > *- behind you*
>
> *And put a sign up*
>
> *Closed to all but me.*
>
> from *Directive,* by Robert Frost

Chapter Three: Transition

I received a letter from a seventy year old friend recently. She expressed a sense of disappointment over the way her life was moving forward. Here are some of her words: "I somehow feel that since I've retired, I've worked hard at getting my act together. Now I feel a sense of failure has been introduced. Why is it that once you've learned the answers, they change the questions? Once you are secure in your role, you find the play is different?"

My friend retired in her early sixties. At that time she knew she was making a major change. She understood that retirement from a successful career called for major changes in her way of living. She was eager to change a work ethic to a leisurely style of life. She traded her work for playing bridge, her research for golf, and she made new friends in what she assumed were in her appropriate age bracket.

Now, after ten years, a shoulder operation stopped her golf, bridge had become increasingly boring, and she was suffering from a sense of disorientation. What next? How could she find a safe haven and a purposeful life in a rapidly changing world?

Transitions are both painful and necessary if we are to cope with a changing world. Transitions represent a time where you find your journey to be at a crossroad. It is a time of mixed signals. Some coming from the past, some from the future. A new narrative beckons while the old narrative tells you to remain with what worked in the past. I replied to her letter by assuring her that what she described were natural feelings of someone on the verge of a transition. When life's plans become unglued, when none of the certainties and absolutes of the past work any longer or even matter, you know you are facing a transition.

Today there is a need for the experiencing of transitions. Without a transition we can become dysfunctional and rapidly retreat into a *bunker* reality. A *bunker* reality is when we hold fast to the old ways without allowing anything new to enter our consciousness. *Bunker* reality seems safe, but it keep us from reaching maturity. Hence we remain oblivious to the changing world.

Some time ago Gail Sheehy described in a book called *Passages* how people grow as they age. She compares the human journey to the life of a lobster. The lobster grows by the development, and then the shedding of a series of hard protective shells. Each time it expands from within by sloughing off a confining shell. During this process the lobster is left exposed and vulnerable.

This period which I have labeled the transition period is illustrative of Sheehy's explanation. It usually comes when we have stumbled, fallen or failed at some of our goals. Suddenly we feel exposed. Our boundaries are ready to be changed, and what we thought was reality, or maybe the right way, or even the truth, is now in question. We are ready to slough off our outer shell, but we feel a sense of anxiety. We feel like a shipwrecked sailor, lost on an uncharted island. It is at this stage that we feel most confused and vulnerable. We would like to say good bye to the old, but are not yet ready for the new.

In order to move from the old narrative to the new it is necessary to go through a transition period. A definition of a transition period is the abandoning of one narrative and the readiness for a new one. As William Bridges wrote in his book, *Transitions:* "The path of development is the fishtailing course we follow as we let go of what we have been and then discover a new thing to become -- only to let go of that in time and become something new." In normal times this can occur gradually, but when there is much turbulence, great changes, rapid movement, we do not have an option. We find what was right five years ago no longer works. What made sense a few years ago looks ridiculous in the light of what we now know. The person we thought we were is no longer present.

Transitions are crucial if we are to take on a new narrative. They are a necessary part of aging but they represent changes that we try to avoid. Our ego is often bound up in our former narratives. If we put aside a chosen narrative, the question always remains: what next? Will it all result in chaos? Will disorientation take over and the unknown lead us into disaster? Moving from an ending to a beginning has both a sense of promise and a sense of despair. It's the in-between zone. It is when you are prepared to let go of your old narrative but haven't fully incorporated a new identity. Something inner is gestating and life seems risky. You can not predict the future.

Arnold van Gennep, a Dutch anthropologist, was the first to interpret these transitions as rites of passage. It was he who pointed out that such rites were the way in which traditional societies structured life transitions. The first phase of a transition was a symbolic death experience. Then came a time which he called the neutral zone. Finally, there was the incorporation into the social order on a new basis. Van Gennep wrote extensively about endings, neutral zones and new beginnings. Transitions to a new narrative certainly mirror his analysis. When you fall, or fail, or simply find that you are faced with a major change and it doesn't fit your narrative, this heralds the beginning of transition. It represents a death experience, the death of an old narrative. Then there is the neutral zone, the exploration of what a new narrative might encompass. Finally there is the incorporation phase of taking on a new narrative. This is usually preceded by some ritual recognition of the change. These ritual ceremonies are the landmarks of human life and differ only in detail from one culture to another, according to van Gennep.

Another way to look at transitions is to see them as segues between the pathways of aging. The Bible uses the term Metanoia which we may translate into repentance. But Metanoia translated simply means to turn around, to become other than we are. This is what a transition is all about. It is a turning around of one's narrative. It's becoming new. Abram becomes Abraham, Saul becomes Paul. It is really not simply something about a new identity as much as it is the recognition of an entirely new narrative.

Stumbling and falling as we go through life's cycle

are not to be viewed as disasters to be averted so much as cues to let go of old narratives and take on new ones. They are often signals that we are in a period of change. For most of us, this produces a feeling of anxiety. Soren Kierkegaard, the Danish philosopher, was once asked to define anxiety. He said very simply--anxiety is the next day. For Kierkegaard the future, the great unknown was the scary part of existence. Letting go, beginning again are easily understood and easily measured in terms of risk and gain, but the neutral zone, where nothing is happening, the future unknown, is an apt description of Kierkegaard's anxiety. As someone once described it, it is like being a circus performer suspended between trapezes, or it's Linus when his blanket is in the dryer. There is nothing to hold on to.

Transitions are times of inner reorientation and personal change. As we age, we need to readjust to changing circumstances. There are times to end one narrative and transition into beginning a new path. This represents unchartered territory. There are no predictable outcomes when one faces a transition moment. Which is why we find it to be so anxiety producing.

One of the most gifted writers America has ever produced was Thomas Wolfe. In the conclusion of his well known book *You can't Go Home Again,* there is a chapter called Ecclesiastics. In it he writes: "The essence of belief is doubt, the essence of reality is questioning. The essence of time is flow not fix. The essence of faith is the knowledge that all flows and that everything must change."

And so it is that transitions are the engines of change. They are the necessary movements that awaken us from one narrative to another. Transitions are when doubts and questions indicate that changes are in the wings. They point out that we have ended one narrative and are ready to begin a new one. If we could recognize these transitions, we might be able to celebrate them as important steps in the afternoon of life.

The real act of discovery consists not of finding new lands, but in seeing with new eyes.

Marcel Proust

Chapter Four: Hardening of the Narrative

All our narratives are tentative. Just as the world changes so does our narrative. Perhaps we should say that, at least, we have the possibility of changing. Our narratives are a way in which we understand reality and truth. Reality and truth change as we grow older or we have had extensive life experiences. As children, we often felt our parents were the last word. As we grew older we found other truths and other authorities. At twenty we might have seen ourselves as immortal, by the time we reach 70, we are aware that death is a serious consideration. It is not that the narrative at any stage of life is wrong. Narratives by definition are incomplete and subject to change.

The psychologist, Dan P. McAdams, describes life journey through personal stories or what he calls myths. We are born, he says, into a family myth that includes what the family knows about itself: where it came from, its place in the neighborhood, the foods it eats, the worldview it espouses. Not until late adolescence do we begin to form our own personal myth, built on the foundation of the family myth but veering off according to our personal preferences. Early adulthood is spent integrating our various selves into the myth as a professional, spouse, or partner, parent, citizen, man, or woman. By middle age we are concerned about our legacy. Have we done enough? Will we be remembered? The final phase in McAdams' scheme, the post myth, occurs when the end of the story is almost in sight. Now the work is not about refining the myth, but about examining it.

This examination is often referred to by clinicians as a life review. If we do this carefully, some will notice that as we aged our narrative stayed the same. What we believed about life at forty remained the same when we reached seventy. What truths we learned at a young age we kept enshrined as we aged. For some this was seen as a virtue, but for others it was an excuse not to explore different narratives and different ways to behave in a changing world. Holding tight to one's narrative can often lead to a hardening of one's point of view. It can lead to a disease called the certainties. The certainties say that my view of reality and truth is the only view that counts. My narrative is THE narrative, my half truth is the only truth. Certainties do not allow for questions or doubts. It is the narrative of the true believer. It can also lead to intolerance and fanaticism. Disintegration sets in when we stop the search for new paths in aging. We are not immune to this hardening of our narratives.

This is the demonic part of narratives. We become prisoners of one narrative or another which often occurs when we fail to transition to the second half of life. We hold tightly to the narrative formed by parents, teachers, or society in general. Part of this narrative is that everything will go according to plan. This is primitive. It presents us with an illusion of safety. As we age, we face failures, insurmountable problems, and disappointments. Inevitably, this sort of narrative falls apart. We find, in the second half of life, a choice of freedom from rigid, outmoded narratives, or we face the possibility of seeing oneself in the same old way. One reason we harden our narratives is that we can remain childlike and drive away the fear of change. We repeat the mantra to ourselves: "This is the way life is supposed to be lived."

I had a friend who was a college professor. He used to say to students who were about to graduate. "Watch it, lest 50 years from now, you look back on the springtime of your life and say, "Ah, those were the days." And find unfortunately you were right."

One reason we tend to stay trapped is the childhood fear of abandonment. Suppose we change and people reject the new you? Another reason is the last thing most of us want is to live with is uncertainty. To change is to risk moving into the unknown. Many of us prefer the security of known misery to the misery of unfamiliar insecurity.

One final reason for being stuck is the belief that someone or something needs to change before we can move forward. This places the responsibility for the hardening of the narrative on an outside factor and relieves us of making a choice.

Ashley Montague, writing many years ago, identified this disease as psychosclerosis, as opposed to arteriosclerosis, the hardening of the arteries. Psycho sclerosis was the hardening of the spirit. As a result of this disease the mind cannot see or embrace new ideas, and the heart cannot stay vulnerable. We automatically reject the need to change and stay stuck or as I would say, "pickled in the past."

In a recent study group the challenge to change was the center of discussion. One participant complained: "We've just gotten used to cell phones and now they want us to carry Blackberries. We don't use all those modern gadgets in our household. What was good enough for my parents is good enough for me." These are signs of a hardening of the narrative. It's not simply a failure to use up to date technology, but rather a sign of narrative paralysis. Hardening comes about when we choose stability over progress, and safety over the unknown, and stagnation over self-discovery.

When does this paralysis take hold? There are three times when this occurs. It happens when the cost of maintaining the old realities rise. It happens when modern thought, for example, has shown the benefits of sharing feeling, and our old narrative tells us that "real men, don't cry." The old narrative says the rules are that we don't show emotions. Then we learn that if we fail to show feelings, bottle up our emotions, this can be costly to our mental health. It happens again when we move to a new location or find the culture different from our familiar workplace. Do we use the old responses that worked in the past, when clearly we are in a different culture? Do we expect the new to be like the old? This can be a huge problem particularly if the past was successful. What worked yesterday can easily become the gilded cage of tomorrow. And finally, when our dreams don't materialize, do we simply hold on to dreams that can never be fulfilled? Do we blame outside factors for our lack of progress? Do we just give up and say "we're just too old to change."

In his perceptive book, *Games people Play*, Dr. Eric Berne describes the too old to change mentality as a way people use different conditions to manipulate situations. He labels it the *wooden leg* theory. The message is what can you expect from someone with a wooden leg or in this case, when faced with a possible shift in narratives, we opt to remain in the old one, and we say: "What can you expect from an old person like myself." This, of course, is a cop-out and keeps us holding on to the past and allowing paralysis to take over.

The struggle between hardening of the narrative and changing the narrative is the critical message of this book. It is my hope that as we reflect on our own narratives, we can locate where we stand in the aging process. As we mature, traveling down one path or another, we can put aside those unhelpful messages that say, "We don't do it that way," or "I wish it were that easy," or "Let's get real," or "That's impossible," or "If only they would act differently." Those responses keep us towing the line of the status quo, and block us from transitions to the new.

There is an ancient Hebrew prayer that goes:

From the cowardness that shirks from new truths; from the laziness that is content with half truths; from the arrogance that thinks it knows all truth, O God of truth deliver us.

Chapter Five: Narrative Shifts

A good measurement of how we might handle narrative shifts in the future is to be aware of how we handled transitions in the past. It is important to realize how we processed information which enabled us to change any of our core beliefs.

To maintain the status quo means staying within your comfort zone. When new experiences or new information comes to us, we often feel uncomfortable. Our ego is tied up with the old narrative, just as our identity is bound up with the assumptions we make about life. We are quite ready to make small changes without upsetting our basic narratives. But small changes will not shift our basic thought process. The problem arises when we face major life style changes. Rilke, the Austrian poet and novelist, reminds us that when we are only victorious over small things, it leaves us feeling small. Small changes do not lead us into shifts of core beliefs. In order to make major shifts in our pathways, we have to learn to accept what is happening and believe that our lives are always evolving. Many people tend to live a core narrative that stopped at middle age. What is important here is the acknowledgement of where we are.

If we are trapped in a hardened narrative, the first step is one of recognition.

The question then can be: what is it that makes us open to moving or changing pathways? What makes us open to changing our narrative as we move through the life cycle? Another way to look at our situation is to ask what do we have to reject in order to move forward?

Most changes start with the heart and not the head. Information alone will not enable change. A good example of this is the story of Ed. He reached the age of 75 without many aches and pains. His doctor told him recently that his habit of four or five cocktails before dinner was not a good idea. This information was duly noted yet he continued in the same pattern. It was part of his life style. He didn't want to disappoint those close to him who had adopted a long *happy hour.* This continued until he became an alcoholic. Information alone, a matter of the head, did not produce change. It was his heart which needed to change. And this could only be done if his narrative were to shift. The way he saw himself needed to be changed. The poet Rilke speaks of Herz-Werk, which is heart work, the journey one makes within the self.

Whenever you are faced with making a change, I would remind you of Don Juan's advice in *The Teachings of Don Juan* by Carlos Castaneda: " I warn you. Look at every path closely and deliberately. Try it as many times as you think necessary. Then ask yourself, and yourself alone, one question. This question is one that only a very old man asks. My benefactor told me about it once when I was young, and my blood was too vigorous for me to understand it. Now I do understand it. I will tell you what it is: Does this path have heart?

The trouble is nobody asks the question; and when a man finally realizes that he has taken a path without a heart, the path is ready to kill him. At that point very few persons can stop to deliberate and leave the path.

For me there is only the traveling on paths that have heart, on any path that may have heart."

I spoke recently with Joe, who told me that he is ready to give up on this business of aging. Joe said: "I've tried all the many tactics on successful aging, read all the books and nothing seems to work." His dreams and even some waking hours are filled with images of death. It's not that he's afraid of death so much as he's fearful of the way he might die. He visualizes himself alone in some hospital bed with a million tubes in him.

All I could reply is that aging isn't for the faint of heart. The secret is having the courage to begin again, to change your narrative, to learn to live in the moment, learning to begin again with a gift of faith.

Elie Weisel, the survivor of the holocaust, put it very clearly when he said: "When He created man God gave him a secret -- and that secret was not how to begin, but how to begin again. It is not given to man to begin; that privilege is God's alone. But it is given to man to begin again --- and he does so every time he chooses to defy death and side with the living."

How do you start over at 80? How do you become new, changed, fresh at 90? It's a curious question for an old man or woman, or maybe it's the only question that older people ought to ask. How is it possible to lay aside all the old bad things we've collected through the years?

To side with the living means to recognize that we can change. We can shift our narratives to fit new circumstances. We may not be able to choose how we die, but we can choose how we live.

Far too often we take a fatalistic stance in life. Whatever will be will be. Again and again we need to be reminded there is another way. We can view aging as a process of becoming. We can begin to ask, what is the work we have to do before we die? If you can begin to see death as an invisible, but friendly companion on your life's journey, gently reminding you not to wait till tomorrow to do what you meant to do. Then you can live your life rather than simply passing through it. The very act of making a shift in one's narrative is an affirmation that there is more to come. Shifting narratives is a way that we ask God to guide us to become closer to what the Creator had in mind for us.

You are called to become--

It does not matter

how short or tall

Or thick-set or slow

You may be

It does not matter

Whether you sparkle with life

Or as silent as a still pool

Whether you sing your song aloud

Or weep alone in darkness.

It does not matter

Whether you feel loved or admired

Or unloved and alone

For you are called to become

A perfect creation

No one's shadow

Should cloud your becoming

No one's light

should dispel your spark

For the Lord delights in you

Jealously looks upon you

And encourages with gentle joy

Every movement of the Spirit

Within you.

Part of a poem called *Called to Become* by Edwina Gateley

Chapter Six: Pathway Narrative: To Be Productive is To Be Fully Alive

As we walk down this pathway narrative, we feel as if we are in control of our lives and the immediate future is relatively predictable. As one man in a class on aging said. "Old age is a conspiracy that the economic world has fostered upon a gullible public. I'm going to decide when it's right to join the ranks of the elderly."

We still believe at this stage that exercise, vitamins, and rest can beat the aging process. To get old is a production of the mind. You can control this so called reality. Self-determination, hard work, and planning ahead are the keys to living the good life. We believe that we are viewed by the world by the choices we make. Another participant said: "If you want to walk around with a cane and your hair in a bun, and old folk clothes, that is your choice. But I choose to keep in style." This pathway is sometimes referred to as the time of Botox, face lifts, macrobiotic diets, and personal trainers.

The primary emotions within this pathway are denial, optimism and anger. We find our energy directed toward resisting labels like senior citizen, and elderly.

Our intellect tells us that we are going to die, but we put off thinking about it. As Woody Allen once said: "I'm not afraid of dying, I just don't want to be there when it happens."

Ernest Becker in his book, *The Denial of Death*, writes "We human beings are caught in a tragic situation. We are aware of our potential for grandeur, and yet we also know that in a few short years we will be gone." Somehow we have to hold both of these realities together. In fact Becker adds, "What drives most of us is terror and anxiety that comes from the fact that we know how fragile life is. And so we set about our anxious projects for finding security, leaving our mark, and proving our worth."

Sometimes, along this path, we are willing to try a new career. At the same time we hold tightly to the traditions and ways of operating that worked in the past. One of the story lines for this narrative is: "You can't teach an old dog new tricks." Another story line is: "If it worked in the past, it will work in the future." We believe, that one's chronological age doesn't matter, although we may admit that we have slowed down a step or two. Many on this path refuse to consider retirement. But even if we are retired, we still feel a need to be productive.

Marc Freedman, CEO and founder of Encore.org, a

website dedicated to helping those who are approaching retirement, recommends embarking on a second act in aging. "Increasingly we'll see people who have multiple working chapters, including one that began in the 70's. It doesn't make sense to work like a maniac for 30 years and be put out to pasture for a period that could be that long in duration."

Our faith journeys are fairly routine. We continue in the patterns of worship that worked in the past. We are comfortable in saying our prayers with people of like mind. We react strongly at changes that seem to question traditional beliefs. Richard Rohr, the insightful writer who is also a Roman Catholic priest, talks about the crab bucket syndrome during this pathway. He pictures a crab trying to get out of a bucket filled with other crabs who keep pulling him back in. This is true of many of our assumptions at this stage. We have found it easier to go along with what the general culture assumes about the good life. Even when a new reality is presented and seems to have promise, we are pulled back to the old ways by what the general consensus seems to be. Whenever we are faced with new ideas, we see them as radical. We would like to establish a sense of permanence. We find ourselves saying, "We don't do things that way." The traditional and the tried and true ways are good enough.

Thomas Merton, the well-known monk, pointed out that at this stage many have spent so much time and energy in building their personal salvation projects that they will do most anything to hold on to it. Most people seem to agree that the lessons we learned in Kindergarten or Sunday School are still applicable today. You feel that the present religious scene has gotten away from the basics and that is why it's declining. You uphold vigorously those who would turn back the clock. You mourn the loss of traditional thinking. You resist some of the new technology and hope you will not be forced to use all the stuff that the younger generation treats as normal. You pride yourself as one who exists in the modern world with old-fashioned ideas.

What we call the beginning is often the end. And to make a beginning, the end is where we start from.

T.S. Eliot *Four Quartets*

Chapter Seven: Pathway Narrative: The Way of New-found Freedom

You find yourself open to a new career or a new hobby. Aging is seen as an opportunity to try some new behaviors. You recognize that the world is rapidly changing and you want to change with the new day. You are very much aware that you possess many unused talents and skills that have not surfaced in the past.

You have become mindful that you are free to write your own narrative. What you have said *yes* to in middle years is not applicable in later life. As someone once said: "machines are consistent, people are not. They only try to be." It's unfortunately true that most people don't take enough responsibility for their own narratives. They would rather stay with the narrative handed to them by society. They tend to live out the scripts which other people have written for them. You have determined that this kind of a narrative is not your cup of tea. What you really want is freedom and safety, but these are strange bedfellows. Freedom is not to be confused with liberty. Freedom is not doing your own thing. Freedom in this narrative means that you are the author of your own experience. You feel it is imperative to set your own course as you age. As Edna Ferber wrote: "Some people make the world, the rest just come along and live in it." You want to have a hand in forming your own world. This has some good and bad news. Choosing this pathway means you surrender innocence and exchange it for guilt. You have made the choice of this narrative, therefore you are accountable.

You are very cognizant of people who, in the afternoon of life, did impressive things. Michelangelo was chief architect of St. Peter's Basilica between the ages of 71-89. Grandma Moses took up painting when she was 78. Miriam Hart flew solo across the Atlantic at 84.

There is a sense of adventure in this pathway. Hobbies and extra curricular skills become important. The opportunity to mentor people and pass on your experience to the younger generation has a serious pull. As the last step of *Alcoholics Anonymous* tells us, a person must pass on the lessons learned or there has been no real learning.

In a *New York Times* article (Sunday March 9, 2014) Arts and Leisure section, entitled, *Domingo Undimmed*, Michael Cooper wrote; "the famous singer Placido Domingo vaulting from one stage to the next, the opera's eternal man defies his age. He has been defying the gravity of age and continuing to command the stages of the world's opera houses and as a result is recognized as one of the more remarkable transformations in opera history. Mr. Domingo one of the great tenors of recent memory is making a second career singing baritone roles."

You embrace change as it emerges from the shadows and see yourself transforming your life. You have what is sometimes called a beginner's mind. In Japan there is a phrase *shoshin*, which means your mind is empty and ready for anything. You are constantly open to new possibilities. In the beginner's mind there are many possibilities, in the dilettante's mind there are few. At this age some people are preparing to sound taps. You are ready to blow reveille.

At the same time you are quite concerned with your own legacy. How will you be remembered? Somehow you would like to omit mistakes and be remembered for the good you accomplished. You wonder what will survive the test of time? There is a great deal of soul searching in this pathway. You would like to recreate some relationships, erase some decisions, and begin again in some areas.

Your faith journey is one of action. You are concerned with many of the problems of the world and feel called to do something to alleviate suffering. You choose to be a part of a community that accomplishes good works. You are not so much concerned with attendance at worship as with serving others. You have developed a skeptical attitude toward many of the rules and regulations of your childhood faith. The only rule that you recognize is to do what is most loving in any situation. When you violate the opportunity to act in a loving manner, you feel a strong sense of guilt.

This pathway is characterized by a sense of hard reality. Life is difficult and we are our own worst enemies when we deny it. Self-disclosure is a high value, and truth telling is prized as a form of communication. You are not so much concerned with who is doing what, but are painfully aware when you fail to live up to your ideals. This narrative believes that what you see is what you get. And what you get is what you deserve.

Lord, thou knowest better than I know myself that I am growing older and will some day be old. Keep me from the fatal habit of thinking I must say something on every subject and on every occasion. Release me from craving to straighten out everybody's affairs. Make me thoughtful but not moody, helpful abut not bossy. With my vast store of wisdom, it seems a pity not to use it all, but thou knowest, Lord, that I want a few friends at the end.

Seal my lips on my aches and pains. They are increasing, and love of rehearsing them is becoming increasing sweeter as the years go by. Give me the ability to see good things in unexpected places, and talents in unexpected people. And give me, O Lord, the grace to tell them so. Amen

An anonymous 17th century nun's prayer

Chapter Eight: Pathway Narrative: Learning to Set Limits

In this pathway we learn to make the best use of failing resources. As we age, health, finances, and what we have earned are being eaten away. We are aware of limitations. We recognize that the world defines us by age. We are mindful that we are part of a generation, not just a lone individual who "rages against the dying light." The fact of mortality is accepted slowly. You are particularly cognizant of people close to you who die or move away. As these people leave, this question seems to echo in your mind: "If you walk out of my life can I go on without you?"

You are in the process of paring down to essentials. You find yourself planning what to give away and what to leave for future generations. You have fewer friends, but those you have kept are closer.

You practice better stewardship because you have less resources. You have little need to buy the latest thing, but appreciate what you have. Anthony de Mello writes: "Happiness is dropping attachments, desires and illusions."

You are aware of the feelings of being put out to pasture, out of sight, and out of mind. In spite of society's assumptions, you are learning to appreciate that you have more time to concentrate on a few important things and to ignore the cultural message. You have learned a valuable lesson. You have learned to keep yourself company.

As you go deeper into this pathway, you are able to move from being a victim of the aging process to a survivor. Many people never stop to realize that they have survived. No one promised us a rose garden. Aging is not easy. It seems to creep up on us so quickly. And just because you have reached some magic age, it does not guarantee that life will be smooth sailing. Instead, some continue to cast blame on the world, the job, or fate for their condition. If one continues the *blame game,* the question will not be asked: for what purpose have I survived? In order to find answers, we must move deeper into the inner journey and wrestle with what is real as we face a changing rapidly world.

There is a great sense of liberation along this pathway of setting limits. Coupled with the concern of losing things, there is also the knowledge that, in the process, we haven't disintegrated. Within every situation of loss there stands the possibility of gain. Carl Jung said it so well when he wrote: "Where you stumble and fall, there you will find true gold." We may cringe at thinking about how we have to wind down but within this narrative we can also be assured that we can find time and space for new possibilities.

You are beginning to shrug off many of the values and rules of younger years in this faith journey. You have been able to shed the myth of total control. You are just coming to terms with the fact that this is God's world. You are beginning to question what is it that God wants you to do in your remaining time on earth? In this pathway you discover inner resources that make some of the older boundaries irrelevant. Roles and rules that seemed important years back no longer hold sway. You are more willing to confront long held assumptions, without abandoning whatever faith community was relevant in the past. The search is more important than the answers. You are more willing to live with the questions.

The Austrian poet Rilke captures this attitude when he wrote: "Be patient with all that is unsolved in your heart, and try to love the questions themselves. Do not seek the answers that cannot be given you because you would not be able to live them. And the point is to live everything. Live the questions now. Perhaps you will then gradually, without noticing it, some distant day live into the answers." Good questions work on us. We don't work on them. They are not a project to be completed, but a doorway opening onto a greater depth of understanding.

It's important to come to terms with the years ahead. Now that you have substituted the anguish of searching for the arrogance of easy answers, you can look ahead without the anxiety of having to solve everything immediately. You have survived the first sixty years, what are you going to do with the next ten, twenty, or even thirty years?

In order to move in this pathway you must cease asking what is wrong with you. Acknowledge what is happening and be ready to move on. In this way you can learn to appreciate the time you have left. You can do this by viewing problems as signals to let go, to stop seeing failures as problems to be solved or removed. These all can be taken as signals that you are ready for a transition.

In this narrative you are more and more aware of keeping yourself company. Wallace Stevens pointed out "that at this time of his life, You no longer need to sky dive, run a marathon, or play 36 holes of golf, you now take pleasure in circulating." Stevens reference to circulating is the lost art of being a friend and touching peoples lives

Added to *circulating* are times of solitary intimacy. Meditation, prayer and reflection times are seen as important parts of your faith journey. Having a conversation with oneself is a rare gift that one practices during this pathway. There is more pressure to find inner authority or inner resources than at other times in one's life. You realize as Jeremiah said: "But this is the covenant that I will make with the house of Israel: After those days; says the Lord. I will put my law in their minds, and write it on their hearts." Somehow you are finding the prayers you said with your lips are taking hold in your heart. What was formerly seen as impediments to growth are now viewed as stepping stones to a broader view of creation. What was seen as stumbling and falling down is now viewed as part of a sacred dance. It need not be overlooked.

When death comes like an iceberg

between the shoulder blades

I want to step through the door

full of curiosity, wondering:

what is it going to be like, that

cottage of darkness?

And therefore I look upon everything

as a brotherhood and a sisterhood,

and I look upon time as no more

than an idea,

and I consider eternity as another

possibility,...

When it's over, I want to say: all my life

I was a bride married to amazement.

I was the bridegroom, taking the

world into my arms.

When it's over, I don't want to wonder

if I have made my life something

particular, and real.

I don't want to find myself sighing

and frightened, or full of argument.

I don't want to end up simply

having visited this world.

An excerpt from *When Death Comes*, by Mary Oliver

Chapter Nine: Pathway Narrative: Living With Imperfection

You are able to choose maturity over wisdom as you travel this pathway. Wisdom is the accumulation of knowledge and the experience that comes with age. Maturity means living with ambiguity; where forgiveness is more important than being right, and relationships are more important than reputation. Maturity also means that you take risks and you raise those difficult questions. As Einstein was quoted: "Imagination is more important than knowledge. It is not enough to analyze the world as it is and ask why. We need also to imagine the world as it might be and ask why not."

You are able to view failures, loss , and mistakes through a different lens. Perhaps what looks like a negative can be seen as positive. In the dark times you are able to find meaning. Professor John Finley of Harvard defined maturity at this stage as the capacity to live with uncertainty. The very act of stumbling can be seen in a broader context. Questioning the answers of the past is a necessary step in transition. Maturity, not perfection, is the goal of this path. The task of aging is to make peace with the burdens of the past and raise questions about what the future holds.

One of the most difficult tasks of this path is learning to say goodbye to things before you are able to say hello to others. Sometimes this means saying goodbye to people. At other times it means saying goodbye to hurts and anger and perhaps even some dreams. There are also feelings of guilt when faced with saying goodbye to friends and family and feelings that we could have done more, along with the awareness of lost opportunities.

There is a sense of incompleteness deep down inside most of us. Everything may appear smooth on the surface, but we all know there are gaps down inside. In each of us there are painful memories, parts of our lives that need reconciliation, holes to be filled. Somehow during this pathway we find holes can be filled and gaps brought together. This is the pathway where forgiveness is found and where we stumble, then we find the strength to keep going forward.

Nikos Kozantakos, in one of his books, describes this path. He tells of a medieval peasant who asked a monk what the holy fathers did behind the walls of the monastery. Such a place was close to heaven itself in his eyes. But the monk with great wisdom answered simply, "Well, we fall down and we get up. And we fall down and we get up."

In this pathway you find constant challenges to leave your comfort zone, take risks, learn to trust, remain open in a world that teaches that winning is everything and being powerful are measures of a life well lived. Maturity calls for a re-evaluation of what our prior thoughts were to the answers of life. Maturity looks at who we are and not what we do and how we try regardless of whether or not we succeed. Maturity has taught us that if a thing is worth doing, it is worth doing badly. You don't have to go for perfection. You are valuable because of what you are and not because of what you do.

In this pathway there is a keen sense of self validation. You do not feel the need to be recognized by others. Directions are taken from within. It is a great feeling of not having to seek permission from outside authorities. Your life is self directed or as Jung has indicated: you now have a sense of *individuation*. This happens as a result of multiple experiences of loss and separation.

G.B. Shaw in a wise statement said: "The British people's greatest delusion was that they felt they had read *The Origin of the Species*. If they had really understood it, they would not talk about survival of the fittest. The phrase does not refer to survival of the most powerful. It means the direct opposite. Only those forms of life survive that are capable of coping with a changing environment."

As David, one of the class of 80 year old seniors who were exploring change, said: "My expectations of what I can gain from life has changed. The world no longer owes me anything, therefore whatever happens is a plus. I am not dependent on the affirmation of others. I am learning to accept and cope with whatever is to be."

This pathway is rich in possibilities. We can unlearn foibles of a lifetime, see through our self-deceptions, and gain a deeper understanding of compassion.

You might have felt resentment about being retired in former times.. Now you see it as a gift where you can make major shifts of priorities and do not have to answer for what you would like to do. You can now spend time doing some of the things that have been put aside. You can even be reckless in your loving of others, no longer with the worry of whether it's reciprocated. You can show acts of caring even when the recipient doesn't deserve your compassion. You now see forgiveness in a different light You thought of forgiveness as an act of forgetting, or not demanding full restitution. Now your understanding is closer to the original Greek word. In Greek the word *forgiveness* means to release, to let go, to surrender. For you, forgiveness is a profound act of letting go.

Nothing that is worth doing can be achieved in our lifetime; therefore we must be saved by hope. Nothing which is true or beautiful or good makes complete sense in any immediate context of history; therefore we must be saved by faith. Nothing we do, however virtuous, can be accomplished alone; therefore we must be saved by love. No virtuous act is quite as virtuous from the standpoint of our friend or foe as from our own standpoint. Therefore we must be saved by that final form of love, which is forgiveness.

The Irony of American History, Reinhold Niebuhr

Chapter Ten: Pathway Narrative: Living In The Now and Not Yet

As the pathway changes, you are conscious of movement from victim to survivor, and then to one who thrives in the role of elderly. Your life is filled with surprises. You are comfortable in your own skin even though that skin is wrinkled. You are at ease with being old. The *not-yet* elicits no fear. The now is filled with moments of joy.

If you never mature into old age, ignoring the pain and discomfort that aging brings this narrative is not for you. Only those who have searched below the surface, known the blessing of forgiveness, tasted the joy of surrender, and the laughter of being free, can walk this pathway.

It is often asked of people who are in this pathway: Are you concerned about the end of life? They smile, maybe even laugh when people question them about *the after life.* They say its like E.L Doctorow when asked about his novels and whether he had the entire plot clearly in mind and the ending figured out? Doctorow said: "writing a novel is like driving a car at night. You can only see as far as your headlights, but you can make the whole trip that way." So if you can only see a few feet in front of you, on the pathway, maybe that's enough. If your journey is made with faith, you are ready to be surprised. You don't have to have the full picture.

You are optimistic about the future without knowing the whole story. There is a sense of peace. You have traded the many questions you initially had for a sense of gratitude. You are surprised by the simplicity of it all as you put aside the deeper question. Each moment is precious and each change brings you closer to home. You need not be afraid of not knowing more about death and what is to come. You now know that you don't need to know more than you do. Death is just the last letting go. You have discovered that people become something new by saying goodbye to long cherished prejudices and view points. You can look at the past with gratitude for all that happened and with curiosity look forward to what is to come. Dag Hammarskjold in his wonderful memoirs *Markings* wrote: "For all that has been, thanks. For all that shall be, yes."

In your faith journey, you are now ready to return to your childhood faith, but in a different way. You see yourself as part of a long history of faithful people. You don't question the Bible so much as you see yourself as a part of the Scripture's story. Abraham and Paul, Sara and Mary are your role models. The failures of your community are now God's problem, and you feel no compunction to fix them. In some strange way you feel like you are a part of the eternal flow. You may find your body weaker, but the flame within your heart is stronger. You now can appreciate what St. Paul said in 2nd Corinthians; "It is when I am weak then I am strong." Your very weakness are signs of your homecoming. You can rejoice in the *not yet*.

In the past you have learned to handle small losses, now you know that you are not alone in facing the future. You can affirm that God is with you always, and the two of you together walk that lonesome road. As a terminally ill women named Sally said to me when asked about the future. "I need to go with God into death and I am ready, if He is."

Returning to our thoughts on the faith journey. In Moses quest for the promised land, we read that he never reaches it. But the later part of his life was shaped by the knowledge that he walked with God. Even though he died with the journey still underway, Moses knew God walked ahead of him. In this narrative we know no more now than we ever did about the far side of death. We know it's the last letting go, but we begin to know that we don't need to know, and that we need not be afraid of not knowing. God knows and that's all that matters.

Our security lies in the knowledge of God's love that will be with us always.

And did you get what

you wanted from life, even as

I did.

And what did you want

To call myself beloved, to feel

Myself beloved on the earth

Raymond Carter *Fires* 1989 New York Vintage-Random House

Chapter Eleven: What if, how long and how much?

As we age, most of us live in the land of *What if.* What if we could change our narrative? What if there were other ways to solve the problems of aging?

The underlying assumption of this book is that we need not stop the *what ifs.* You are not encoded genetically with only one way to age. You can change your narrative, and you can do it now. You need only to look around and see how people cope in many different ways with the second half of life. What may seem as irrational or the wrong way to handle the problems of aging may simply be that you are observing a person who has chosen a different narrative.

It takes more than wishes to make changes in our lives. Knowing what we would like to happen doesn't necessarily mean it will happen. To be successful in the afternoon of life, we need more than good intentions.

Many years ago I started a sermon by saying, "I find that I am committed to a lot of things. I'm committed to a diet, to exercise, to study," and the list went on. "The problem," I said, "was my commitment to my commitments." It is easy to speak about commitments. It is hard to follow through when we are pressed for time or the cost is too great.

Instead of choosing to change our narratives, we may look for ways to postpone the whole process. We realize instinctively that it is hard work to make the transition to the aging process. "What's the urgency?" we ask. Maybe we can leave the business of aging for a more convenient time. Others say we have to read one more book, attend one more workshop, need one more lesson on managing aging before we can think about changing.

Unfortunately, sooner or later often adds up to never. The deepest tragedies are not the wrong paths we take. The deepest tragedies are our unwillingness to take risks, to move forward, and to commit fully to the exploration of the wonder-filled afternoon of life.

Some of the most common ways of postponing commitment are raising questions of *how* and *what*. How long will it take to reach maturity? What will it cost?

For those who look for easy answers, the *how long* is a natural. We tell ourselves that we don't have the time to wander through the different paths and look for transitions. We wonder if there isn't some abridged version; can't we pick up a short copy of *Aging for Dummies*?

When we say something takes too long, it usually means that it is not a high priority. We find we have all the time for what is really important. So the question of time shifts to what IS IMPORTANT. What makes us say yes, in the face of all our doubts and fears? Where are our commitments?

Eric Berne, a psychologist who was popular a number of years ago, wrote that the two most important words in the English language were yes and no. He was writing about the choices and decisions that we make in life. Yes stood for those things that we were committed to and no for those we reject. Aging is a process in which we are constantly faced with a yes or a no decision. We say yes to those things that are important, to what we believe to be true, to those actions to which we choose to be accountable. We say no to those forces which would make us dependent on others, giving simple answers to complex questions, and the suggestion that leisure alone is the goal of the second half of life.

Let's be honest, aging for most presents a dilemma. To admit you are old and face your mortality presents us with a crises. Victor Frankl, the psychiatrist who survived the Nazi concentration camp, has suggested that when faced with a crisis people do one of three things. They deny it saying, "aging is really not that bad." They despair saying, "there's nothing anyone can do about it. We'll just have to live with it." Finally they can commit by asking the question of cost and its meaning.

The cost can be a profound question. In our consumer society everything has a price. We may not be able to place an economic value on the changes we make, but they certainly have an emotional cost. Our anxiety level might rise, we may court rejection, and we may face some difficult decisions. One of life's enduring lessons is that which is most valuable cannot be purchased at a discount. Committing to change is a crisis point in our lives. It asks the question: Upon what narrative are you willing to give priority? This will determine how you live the rest of your life.

The price for changing one's narrative may include feeling like a stranger, out of place, living in a foreign land. People often think changing ones narrative is as easy as putting on a new coat. Someone said to me, "I've been feeling down lately. I think I'll just change my narrative." Changing one's narrative is not necessarily a panacea for all problems. The process of change calls for long and difficult internal conversations. It calls for a willingness to face loss and failure, as well as pain and anxiety. In midlife, success is measured by victories which can be accomplished easily. In the afternoon of life, success is measured by surrender of one's ego. This can be costly.

Stella Resnick, a gestalt therapist, put it this way: "Surrender is not a defeat, nor a loss of power, but rather a skill that can improve with practice." To surrender is to let go, to give up control, and then to just let it happen.

In my experience the *how* and *what* questions are more an indirect expression of our doubts than real curiosity. The very act of asking questions makes us trapped by someone else's answers. This does not mean we cannot learn from others. It is just that asking *how* and *what* is not the best way to learn. We learn best by inventing our own steps. We learn by becoming the author of our own experiences. Where one begins this process is never as important as that one begins. This is what lifts us out of the audience mode onto the stage, from an onlooker to a participant. To begin the discovery of your narrative and the willingness to transition to a new pathway means that you are no longer a spectator of the aging process. You have become a player in the movement towards maturity.

The purpose of presenting five pathways is to help you articulate where you stand in the aging process. The five pathways are not exclusive, nor are they necessarily in any sequence. There is no one way which leads one to maturity. Some will invent their own pathways which are different from what has been presented. Some will go back and forth in a more circuitous route. The important point is to begin the conversation. Where you start and where you end is one of life's mysteries. All we can suggest is that aging is a process and not a destination. If you simply fall into old age and never start the process, you will never reach that stage of real maturity.

> *We shall not cease from exploration*
>
> *And the end of all our exploring*
>
> *will be to arrive where we started*
>
> *And know the place for the first time*
>
> T.S. Eliot, *Little Giddings* , *Four Quartets*

Chapter Twelve: Maturity

There is the biological age where we mark the years by the number of candles on our birthday cake. There is the social age where we receive membership privileges at a club for retirees. There is the psychological age where we begin the process of forgetfulness. And then there is the spiritual age where we measure our age by how far we have matured. The problem is that some of us prefer to remain childlike.

One of the favorite remarks of the late William Sloan Coffin, Chaplin at Yale University: "You are young only once, but you can be immature indefinitely."

For the most part we find it easier to remain immature. We avoid the struggle that spiritual growth seems to demand. We shop for reassuring answers that fit our narrative rather than searching for narratives that match what we would like to become. We are immature when we hope for a heaven where all our losses will be replaced and all our failures will be erased. We are immature when we wish to live in a leisure village of the soul, where safety and certainty replace the turmoil of this uncertain world. We long to be a child again, to be protected and cared for without the burden of making major changes. We would rather hold on to the fantasy that *they all lived happily ever after* than face the reality of a fallen world. Could this possibly be why we find so many people in their old age who become hard to live with?

But wait, it is possible to grow spiritually and to seek maturity in a world that seems determined for us to remain immature. Every so often someone emerges that points the way. The great Indian spiritual and political leader Mahatma Gandhi's said: "We need to become the change we want to see." I would add that we need to have a narrative that fits what we would like to become. One way to start would be to imagine or to describe what life would be like if this new narrative were to be embraced. This is the course that embraces integrity over despair and maturity over childish fantasies.

A sign of this maturity is the ability to live with uncertainty. To realize that human beings are called to live between the past which cannot be retrieved and a future that is barely discernible.

A sign of this maturity is to reject the siren song of returning to childhood. To realize that loss and failure are not the last word in the aging process.

A sign of this maturity is to remain open and

vulnerable even at the risk of being hurt. Many years ago a song, *The Rose,* spoke to this issue. Here is the first verse.

> *It's the heart afraid of breaking*
>
> *that never learns to dance*
>
> *It's the dream afraid of waking*
>
> *that never takes a chance.*

To be mature is to take chances and maybe learn to dance, The road to maturity is a rocky one. It contains challenges and choices that threaten our fragile egos. In short, we are approaching maturity to the degree we realize the only security in the afternoon of life is to embrace insecurity, choosing the unknown over the return to known childhood.

W. H. Auden wrote that life is like a first-rate opera played by a 10th-rate road company. The great danger is to lose sight of the first-rate opera by expecting too much from the 10th-rate road company. We somehow think if we have all the answers, make all the right choices, avoid all the pitfalls, we will be accepted by the author of this first-rate opera. Maturity means accepting who and what you are. As Carl Jung said: "accepting the little clod that is me." The road to maturity is acceptance of who we are and where we have been, and then taking the next step. As Confucius said: "It does not matter how slow you go, as long as you don't stop."

Maturity is never a destination; it's always a byproduct of the spiritual journey. No one can ever say "I'm fully mature. I've made it in the business of aging." Maturity is the never ending quest that we never fully reach but nevertheless is the goal of successful aging. It comes about when we are fully involved in the process of living and not fixated on our destination. Maturity is to learn and re-learn the lessons that aging teaches. Sometimes when your are close to the end of your journey, you have a clearer insight into this goal. Here is what an unidentified patient at a hospice shared:

> *After a while you learn the subtle difference*
>
> *Between holding and chaining a soul.*
>
> *And you learn that love doesn't mean leaning*
>
> *And company doesn't mean security.*
>
> *And you begin to learn that kisses aren't contracts,*
>
> *And presents aren't promises.*
>
> *And you begin to accept your defeats*
>
> *With your head up and your eyes open.*
>
> *And learn to build all your roads*

On today because tomorrows ground

Is too uncertain for plans, and futures have

A way of falling down in mid-flight..

So you plant your own garden and decorate

Your own soul, instead of waiting

For someone to bring you flowers.

And you learn that you really can endure...

And you really do have worth

And you learn and learn...

With every good-bye you learn.

The business of maturity is the learner's task. It doesn't happen all at once. It consists of the movement through many narratives. It's a never-ending road that stretches as far as life itself. Joseph Campbell said "When you're on a journey and the end keeps getting further and further away. Then you realize the real end is the journey and not the destination."

For the garden is the only place there is, but you can not find it

Until you have looked for it everywhere and found nowhere that is not a desert;

The miracle is the only thing that happens but to

you it will not be apparent,

Until all events have been studied and nothing happens that you cannot explain;

And life is the destiny you are bound to refuse until you have consented to die.

For the Time Being, W. H. Auden

Chapter Thirteen: Authenticity

Soren Kierkegaard, the 19th century theologian, described life as a play in which all of us have different costumes, some grand, some simple, some threadbare. At the end of the play we all take off our costumes and the question for all will be the same---what did we do with the costumes we had been given?

One of the great gifts that comes in the afternoon of life is that we can take the time to reflect upon who we are and what we were meant to be. In other words, what did you do with the costumes you had been given?

In the first half of life we are more concerned with growth, making a name for ourselves, putting on the costume that makes us recognizable. In the second half of life we have the time to ask the questions: who and what have we become?

The reflection process or the internal conversation has some consequences. There is a new-found freedom that comes from dismantling some of our false assumptions about ourselves and about life. Assumptions such as: those that say children must follow in their parents footsteps or happiness comes from having a good bank account, or in order to become spiritual you have first to be religious. Assumptions like these can be put to rest. We understand that these illusions lead to a sense of disillusionment by the time we reach senior citizenship status. This is why in the second half of life we have to push past much of what we learned earlier. We have to be willing to probe the inner messages behind those that society has given us. Another task of reflection is to closely examine oneself. How authentic is the persona that people encounter and the persona that only you can see?

Acknowledging your present condition, even if it is one of confusion and doubt, enables us to strip away some of the roles society has placed upon us. You may appear successful, well adjusted, supremely happy, but deep inside lie fears and anxieties that no one recognizes.

One of the basic teachings of Alcoholics Anonymous is to give up trying to appear what we are not. A.A. stresses that we are to let go self delusions and face who we are and our condition. This is why A.A. insists that you say your name and your condition before speaking. It's the lore of A.A. that you have to start with the authentic you before you can begin to share your walk.

A well-known theatre critic once commented: "Anyone can write a good first act, but what's in the second act really counts." The second half of life calls for endurance and radical honesty. These are talents that don't come naturally. They need to be developed and nurtured as we mature. It's true that we all learn by experience, but some of us are slow learners. We have to go to summer school before we are able to go behind the facades we have so patiently created.

The first step in this process, to quote William Faulkner, is learning to say goodbye to some things before you can say hello to some other things. This means saying goodbye to broken dreams of what might have happened if only things had been different or saying goodbye to the person we were ten years ago. We are what we are and our past can not be changed.

The next step is the search for what hellos are over the horizon. Where is the person that may have been hidden all these years? Eric Erickson coined the phrase, *identity crisis*. This is when we begin to explore who is the real person. This inner conversation doesn't happen overnight. Sometimes it takes many months or it can be a lifetime project. Some feel that the real search occurs only after a severe loss followed by a deep mourning reaction. This exploration of loss can be the way we begin to say hello to a new narrative. When we understand what is happening, we can view loss and the pain that accompanies it as a source of an unintended and unexpected miracle. There is an opportunity for a new life to emerge as we face the end of life.

Carl Jung calls this movement *individuation.* He tells us that it happens only through multiple experiences of separation and loss. It is a movement into responsible autonomy in which one takes signals from within and directs his life from his own center. This is not selfishness...although it can easily slip into it. Individuation is being centered in the self, no longer looking to others for permission, or justification from outside sources. You are what you are and you are transparent in your actions. There is no longer any need to rationalize or apologize for your behavior.

Too often in this competitive world of ours we think that if we work harder, study more, pray longer, meditate unendingly, that a new person would suddenly appear. In the first half of life we learned that the secret of success was to work harder than the next person. This is not so in the second half of life. Life is no longer competitive. You can't win by trying harder. You're only victorious by surrendering. This is particularly so in the spiritual realm. Thomas Merton, one of the giants of the spiritual life wrote: "The spiritual journey is not about trying to be more and more spiritual." We miss the point and waste our time by trying to emulate the great spiritual icons. What the spiritual journey is all about, he says, is "learning to be yourself, fully yourself."

The great danger in life is despair, the giving up on the self that you see and the attempt to be someone you're not. We often fall prey to thinking, "if only I could be like that person." Or sometimes we think, "if only I could live my life over." The learning from the spiritual teachers is that God has placed us where we are. Although we might yearn for a different role, here is where we have been assigned. We've been given this costume to wear and no other.

Elie Wiesel has put it this way; "When we die and we go to heaven, and we meet our maker, our maker is not going to say to us, why didn't you become a Messiah? Why didn't you discover a cure for cancer? The only thing we're going to be asked at that precise moment is why didn't you become more you?"

The true end in life is to find your way to yourself. It's a journey inward. You do not have to prove, or win, or produce, or do anything but to hug yourself and relax and enjoy this wondrous life that God has given you.

Come my way, my truth, my life

Such a way that gives us breath;

Such a truth that ends all strife:

such a life that killeth death.

George Herbert, *The Hymnal* 1982

Chapter Fourteen: The Sacred Dance

Ever since our prehistoric ancestors made signs at the threshold of a newly found cave, we understood that they were a part of a ritual by which they gained courage to enter the unknown. Rituals have been a part of the history of every civilization. As Arnold van Gennep, the anthropologist noted; "rituals are a part of the rites of passage in every community." Rituals are not simply the property of religious institutions. They are found at the beginnings and endings of every culture.

I'm sorry to report that rituals in the United States have fallen on hard times. We are a utilitarian society, which means we always ask the question of use. "What good will it do me?" Ritual in America seems to rank at the top of useless activities. Ritual becomes irrelevant to a culture that is unable to see beyond the limited confines of its own nose.

One of the final tasks of maturation is the reconstruction of rituals. As we mature, our need for rituals becomes more pronounced. We now see rituals as ways to handle losses and transition to new ways. These rituals are not only necessary for saying goodbye to people and things, they prepare us for saying hello to new life. They are ways that we connect with the sacred, as well as maintaining a relationship with our ancestors.

Every so often at a wedding, I find a skeptical groom turning to me to say: "Well, to tell the truth, I didn't much care for a church wedding with all the ritual. But I guess I can't knock it because it seems to anchor me to a long line of people who have done the same thing."

Even for skeptical grooms, rituals have the power to speak to us in a turbulent world where life is uncertain. There is a value in doing something like lighting a candle, holding hands and saying grace, or the blessing of a new home. It may not be done with the knowledge of why or what good will come of it. You do it because your grandparents did it. Rituals demonstrate the connections we have through time and space, and they also have the power to convey meaning and impart courage as we face the unknown future.

Havelock Ellis, the English social scientist, calls rituals the dance of life. Rituals were ways people got in touch with their god. This sacred dance was an essential part of all communities. He points out that you cannot find a single ancient mystery in which there is no dancing.

Even today, in a culture that is decidedly negative

towards rituals, you find some vestiges of these sacred dances at things like graduations, anniversaries, and yes, retirements. When understood as a sacred dance, they connect us in some mysterious way to the ground of our being.

The question then can be raised, how can we introduce or reintroduce these sacred dances into our lives? Some are already present, if not recognized as such. Some we can invent as we go along. Some just happen in the process of aging. What is most needed is the recognition that the sacred is always present. We live in the sacred at every moment. The best analogy is that the sacred is like water for a fish. The fish may not recognize the water, but that is what surrounds it and makes its existence possible.

I spoke with a friend recently, and told him I was writing a book on aging. He asked me, upon about what aspect of aging was I presently focused. I said rituals. "Oh," he said, "You're writing a book for church people." No, I replied, "Rituals are part of the sacred dance that exists whether were in church or at home. The sacred dance takes place whenever we recognize the wonder and glory and specialness of this world of ours. The sacred is not limited to church or church people nor does this dance necessarily happen in church. It begins whenever we recognize God's presence in the midst of creation."

Scripture tries to make this point when in the 139th psalm, the writer asks the rhetorical question: "Where can I go then from your spirit? Or where can I flee from your presence?" He then answers his question: "If I climb up to heaven, you are there; if I make the grave my bed, you are there also. If I take the wings of the morning and dwell in the uttermost parts of the sea. Even there your hand will lead me and your right hand will hold me fast." These words found in the Bible are part of the sacred dance of the psalmist who is able to laugh at the fragility of life and still affirm the sacredness of creation.

The Rev. Kenneth B. Wentzel, a clergyman who wrote about the end of life and hospice ministry, made a statement that I have kept through the years.

"If someone were to ask me what above all else I coveted for my people. I would not want above all else to see them become notable Bible scholars, nor would I hope that they would become genuinely pious and prayerful or virtuous. No, I would consider myself a success of the highest order if my people learned to dance."

In the second half of life we need not despair as we

slip and slide, fail and fall through the years. This is still God's world and we still live within sacred moments. All we need to do is to learn to dance.

Sometimes a movie can teach us way beyond lectures or learned writings. For me, *Zorba the Greek* has been a parable of the second half of life.

The movie is about an Englishman and Zorba who combine to build an enormous slide to bring timber from the mountain to the water. This is a metaphor of how we spend time and energy in constructing our world. We feel this will be our legacy for future generations.

In the movie, the timber was necessary for the survival of the community, so the whole population came to watch and cheer as the first log slid down to the sea. Once again this emphasizes our human need for affirmation as we steer through the difficult passages in the second half of life.

The huge logs begin to slide down the wire. All of a sudden the weight of the logs crushes the slide, and the whole gigantic enterprise collapses. The villagers slowly, dejectedly move away to their homes. Metaphorically this stands for the transition time. The time of saying goodbye to our dreams of *living happily ever after*. This is the neutral zone where we are left amid the wreckage of former narratives.

In the movie, Zorba and his boss sit alone on the beach. The Englishman mumbles, "It's all over." But Zorba stands up, looks at the slide, and begins to laugh. "Why are you laughing," asks the Englishman? "Have you ever seen such a stupendous crash," Zorba replies. There is silence between the two.

Then the Englishman responds: "Zorba, will you teach me to dance?" The two men begin to dance among the ruins, to dance at the sight of their failure.

This is a sacred dance, the celebration of life, the stepping through the gates of heaven into the arms of God. In this dance, you have to stand with your feet planted in reality. In the movie Zorba is enabled to laugh. There is nothing that can be done about the slide; it has fallen. But he still has a future and is able to lean into that future, like a flower leans into the sun. The message of the sacred dance is this: Do not worry about appearing odd or different. Do not be mindful with what is beyond your control. Your dance may not be the same as your neighbors. Don't be concerned over the right steps. Just remember nobody looks natural when they dance. When you cease asking for guarantees and stop demanding certainty, your feet will take care of themselves. Dancing the sacred dance is the clue to maturity in the second half of life.

May all of us learn to dance...

May you be blessed

with vision

in these shadow times.

may light invade the darkness.--

guiding you through

twilight 'till dawn.

and when the dawn breaks

may you find yourself

upon a threshold

may you enter

and go through.

and may you emerge

into the dance

a whole and holy new

sacred dance---

Maureen J Hilliard, SND

Chapter Fifteen: Epilogue

In my own experience of aging, I am very rarely aware of the opportunities for imagining a new narrative. Instead my mind is often preoccupied with the aches and pains that accompany aging. Every so often there is a moment of clarity when I begin to understand those aches and pains, those disappointments and depressions are signs that change is in the wings. While I might be ready for a change in my narrative, it doesn't necessarily mean it will happen. There are many factors beyond our control. We can not control how others will act. We can not control outcomes. The only freedom granted to us is we can control our responses to the present situation. Our inner narrative helps us to understand what has happened and what new things are in store for us.

In retrospect, I can see how the job that I lost helped me to find the work I needed to do. How the road sign marked closed turned me inward toward places I needed to travel. How the losses that felt unbearable forced me to find meaning and support from other people. The experiences were beyond my control, but later they become gold mines on the path to maturity.

Stumbling blocks can become stepping stones if we view them as part of a transition to a new narrative.

About six years ago, I started to have severe shoulder problems. Eventually this necessitated surgery. As a result, I gave up playing tennis, a sport I enjoyed all my life. Once the operation was over, I realized that I had no control over whether to play or not.

A short while later, I realized, given my limitations, that I did have control over what exercises I could pursue. I choose to try golf. I must admit I've always considered golf a foolish and frustrating sport where players chased a small white ball around a beautiful countryside. Little did I know that it would teach me some valuable lessons about aging. What appeared to be a negative situation, became an important laboratory for life.

Once I began to take golf seriously, I learned that there was both an outer and inner game to the sport. The outer game was simply a matter of mastering a series of mechanical moves. The inner game was the more difficult part, for this is played out in your subconscious mind. One definition of the inner game is: "the art of surrendering to the sweet choreography of the dance you share with the game."

Being a slow learner, it took me several years to

understand that the messages we give ourselves as we play the game are similar to what I have been referring to as the inner narrative. The messages are usually much shorter and usually refer to the specific situation. I believe that I would call them story lines on our larger narratives. Also, recently I discovered a truth about control. You cannot control the score or where your ball has landed. The past is past. But you are in charge of the message you give yourself about these two factors.

Using golf as an illustration is not to convince the reader to take up the game. Golf courses are crowded enough. I hope to demonstrate how one might find insight in the most unlikely places. Golf, for me, has become an extended metaphor for the journey we take in the second half of life.

Recently, I took a lesson in putting from our local golf professional. He kept repeating that the secret to good putting was to tell yourself, "You are a great putter." I listened, but I must confess to skepticism. I couldn't imagine giving myself that kind of a message. The difficulty was in what I called *reality*. I could not envision myself as a great or even an adequate putter. I felt trapped between what I called *reality* and a vague wish to improve my putting skill. How true this is of life. We often feel caught between an old narrative and the possibility of something new. If we settle for the old and never change our narrative we usually end up in the same old way.

Many years ago, this lesson was brought home to me by a quote left on a blackboard that Dr. Frank Williams, who wrote the preface to this book, had used in teaching a class. It said: "If you always do what you always did, you'll always get what you always got." This lesson applies to golf as well as life.

Later in the week, I began to ponder why it was so difficult to absorb my golf teacher's advice. As I reflected on the situation, I discovered there was another small voice in the equation. It was that voice that seemed to appear whenever I contemplated transitioning to a new narrative. I called it, at the time, *reality*. But I have come to understand that this so called *reality* can be changed. I now realize what I labeled reality was what I now call, *my resident policeman.* My resident policeman is the voice that says change is impossible, the boundaries have been set and are immovable, you cannot become anything more than you are today, you'll always get what you've always got. The message may vary but the music is always the same. The resident policeman is there to keep us in line. He reminds us that it's safer to stay indoors then risk the unknown.

How then can we deal with this resident policeman? How can we override this small voice that exerts so much power over our lives? I'm tempted to do what many of our popular novelists are doing. Simply end and suggest that the reader purchase my next book.

In lieu of that answer, let me suggest a way to start. Commit oneself to the process of change. Take the wraps off of your imagination, and then be prepared to follow the road of living and dying, dying and living to new narratives. This can only be done with total commitment.

Without a sense of commitment you experience what the Navajo people describe as the *floating cloud* effect. They speak of having a vision and then it disappears like a cloud. After reading this book, you might attempt to find a new narrative for yourself. You might even imagine what it would be like, but without a sense of commitment, it disappears. Without an outward action, some ritual which signifies to yourself that you are about to take a step into the unknown, all that you have projected will fade away. So take heart, join the dance, and enjoy the journey.

P.S. I went and bought a new putter.

One day you finally knew

what you had to do, and began,
though the voices around you
kept shouting
their bad advice --
though the whole house
began to tremble
and you felt the old tug
at your ankles.
"Mend my life!"
each voice cried.
But you didn't stop.
You knew what you had to do,
though the wind pried
with its stiff fingers
at the very foundations,
though their melancholy
was terrible.
It was already late
enough, and a wild night,
and the road full of fallen
branches and stones.
But little by little,
as you left their voices behind,
the stars began to burn
through the sheets of clouds,
and there was a new voice

which you slowly

recognized as your own,

that kept you company

as you strode deeper and deeper

into the world,

determined to do

the only thing you could do --

determined to save

the only life you could save.

Mary Oliver, *The Journey*

Notes

Introduction

    1. The Collected Works of C. G. Jung

    2. T*he New York Times*, Thursday March 13, 2014
Why Older Often Means Wiser

Chapter One

    1. Betty Freidan, *The Fountain of Age*

    2. Isak Dinesen, *Seven Gothic Tales*

Chapter Two

    1. Gen. 12:1

    2. Flannery O'Conner, *The Habit of Being*

    3. C. G. Jung, *The Collected Works of C. G. Jung*

Chapter Three

    1. Arnold van Gennep, *The Rites of Passage*

Chapter Four

    1. Dan McAdams, *Life Story Model of Identity*

Chapter Eight

    1. Anthony de Mello, *Awareness*

2. Jeremiah 31:3

3. R. M. Rilke, *Letter to a young poet*

Chapter Nine

1. Nikos Kazantzakis, *Report to Greco*

Chapter Eleven

1.Eric Berne, *Games People Play*

Chapter Twelve

1. *A Joseph Campbell Collection*

Chapter Thirteen

1. Thomas Merton, *Thoughts on Solitude*

2. Elie Wiesel, *Souls on Fire*

Chapter Fourteen

1. Psalm 139:7-10

2. Havelock Ellis, *The Dance of Life*

Chapter Fifteen

1. Pia Nilsson and Lynn Marriott, with Ron Sirak, *Play Your Best Golf Now*

Acknowledgement

I am indebted to Dr. James Kelley whose magic with the computer made this book possible. Finally, to Peggy whose loving patience has graced my life and nurtured my transitions.

www.ingramcontent.com/pod-product-compliance
Lightning Source LLC
Chambersburg PA
CBHW070537290526
45790CB00002B/540

Policies, Procedures & Protocols
Of The National Republic

FIRST EDITION
March 2011

I0428579

Copyright © 2011
by
David E. Robinson

Attorney General pro tem
for the Maine Republic free state

MAINE-PATRIOT.com
3 Linnell Circle
Brunswick, Maine 04011

maine-patriot.com

Policy, Procedures & Protocols

"Ye shall know the truth and the truth shall make you free." - *John 8:32.*

Policy, Procedures & Protocols

Policies, Procedures & Protocols

Contents

Policy, Procedures & Protocols

Introduction

Look up the word **sovereign** in several dictionaries. Look for the definitions that fit what the Americans had in mind when they wrote the **Declaration of Independence.**

In the "Consolidated Webster Encyclopedic Dictionary" of 1939, the derivation of the word **sovereign** is as follows: **souverain,** from **superanus; super; above; over.**

The English purposely added the **"g"** and changed the spelling of the word into **sovereign** so that it would include the word **"reign".** The word was also spelled **"sovran"** where the **"e"** has been dropped (*Miriam Webster's Collegiate Dictionary, Tenth Edition*). In the Random House College Dictionary (1984) the word has been further broken down.

My conclusion is that the word **"sovereign"** has been wrongly influenced by the English derivation, and the **true root definition** means **"over and above,"** and that the word should be spelled **"soveran"** (*sov-e-ran*) not **sovereign** and not **sovran.**

So, I am making a big leap here by *declaring* **"soveran"** *to be an* **American word,** — and that we can spell our words the way we want to, and use them to communicate what we want to communicate.

Soveran: *n. - over and above; having supreme authority; dominion; rule, rank or power over; beyond jurisdiction; independent and self-governing; autonomous; potent and unlimited in extent.* **A Soveran is sovereign.**

Can a *"Soveran"* be under any laws, statutes, or "other authority than God"? No. *A "Soveran" is bound only to what he has said; only to his own words.*

If a *"Soveran"* says that he is under a law, or authority — then of course, he is under the very authority of which he speaks.

You may be saying to yourself *"...this is too simple, it can't work this simply!"*

All I have to say is — fine! Have it your way!

You can have it however you like because the choice is yours. **You are the *"Soveran"* in your life.** You have dominion.

You speak your own circumstance! So be careful what you say.

1
What You See Counts

Explorers were in route to the New World; sailing around the tip of Africa in massive ships driven by large canvas sails. They anchored their ships a safe distance off-shore and used open long boats to row a small crew ashore.

Never having seen white men nor their ships before, the natives asked the men how they arrived in that part of the world. The sailors pointed to the ships anchored offshore with their large white sails.

The natives looked in that direction, and no matter how hard the natives tried, they could not see the ships apart from the clouds.

The Shaman of the tribe began to try something new.

In looking at things differently, the image of the ships began to appear in his view. As he began to see things this way, *others* began to "see" the ships too. Within a brief period of time, *everyone* in the tribe could see the ships — *even those who were not there to meet the crew as they rowed ashore.*

The tribe had learned a **new way** to "see" (perceive), and in doing so, extended the boundaries of their world!

"Elisha prayed, and said, Lord, I pray thee, open (my servant's) eyes, that he may see. And the Lord opened the eyes of the young man; and he saw: and, behold, the mountain was full of horses and chariots of fire round about Elisha." — II Kings 6:17.

It becomes increasingly important now, more than ever, that your beliefs be not limited by what you have been taught. You are learning to trust yourself, your own feelings, and the process of your life.

In this world you have choices and free will.

You have the opportunity to realize your full potential as a divine expression of your creator, *to become a creator yourself,* by being aware of the power of righteous thought. Thoughts are **"things";** not just pictures in your mind or sensations in your body.

As you think, you create. Is there ever a time when you're not thinking? You are forever creating your experience with your thoughts!

"As a man thinketh in his heart so is he." — Proverbs 23:7.

You do not have to know the intricacies of the mind – only the ability to use them as they are designed. You can just **"be,"** in the purity of your good intentions.

This is the beauty of life.

You may choose to know more if you wish, or just **"be"** in your experience, and the outcome will remain the same. The ability to create as a child of God is a skill available to everyone!

This is the lesson of native Africans and the Explorers mentioned at the beginning of this report.

Everything that you experience is part of your journey home: your *"return."*

Don't be penalized for *"...failing to make a return."* **You are a child of God.**

2
What Is Really Real?

Today our society - all of it - is based on a fiction.

Fictitious plaintiffs (UNITED STATES) versus fictitious defendants (JOHN DOE) in fictitious courts with *non-consensual* fictitious laws (statutes). Fictitious contracts (DEEDS OF TRUST) are made by fictitious parties, granting fictitious property (TITLES and LEGAL DESCRIPTIONS) to other fictitious parties.

You may say, "I want only the real thing; something that is real."

Real: - *(same root as Republic) - actually being or existing; not fictitious or imaginary; genuine; not artificial, counterfeit or fictitious; not affected; not assumed.*

But what is real? Is matter or even your body real — or are they a composite of thought particles and sound waves with **agreed upon** electromagnetic energies that vibrate in fluctuating patterns so as to reflect light, thus giving the *illusion* of varying degrees of solidity, light, color and motion? **Whew!**

Let's go to the MATRIX where Morpheus introduced Neo to the **"construct."**

Morpheus: "Your appearance is what we call residual *self image* — the mental projection of your digital self."
Neo: "Is this real?

Morpheus: "What is real? How do you define real? If you are talking about what you can feel, what you can taste, what you can see, then *real* is simply **electrical signals interpreted by your mind**."

Does this idea sound familiar? Have you ever heard of this concept before?

*"And God said, **Let us make man in our image, after our likeness**." — Genesis 1:26.*

Man: *- adam - of the earth, hypocrite.*
Image: *- to shade, a phantom, **illusion**, resemblance, **a representative figure**, an idol, a vain show.*

How is it, that by saying you are a "man" you are being a hypocrite?

Hypocrite: *- hypocrisis, the playing of a part on a stage, simulation, to feign, - to separate and put under, the act or practice of simulating or feigning to be what one is not; especially **the assuming of a false appearance**.*

Have we been looking at God and man from the wrong prospective? Are you a creation, an illusion, a representative "figure of the earth"? Is the body real or is it only an "image," a vain show, a reflection of what is in **your mind** (**Mind, God**)?

Morpheous: "The world exists as a neural interactive simulation. You've been living in a Dream world, Neo!"

When Neo was in the "jump program" where he was going to jump across to the other skyscraper, he let his doubt overcome him and he fell. Afterwards he was in pain, and commented to Morpheus, "I thought it wasn't real."

Morpheus: "Your mind *makes* it real; your body cannot live without the mind."

Wait a minute! If there really is nothing real — then what really is real? Really! Well, you know that **you are real** don't you? — *not your body* — just you! Once you have that stable datum, then *you can create reality* with your mind. Not by trying, or wishing, or hoping, or thinking, or even *believing* something into existence — these words are way too *wimpy.* **One must create reality by *KNOWING*!**

"Ye shall KNOW the truth, and the truth shall make you free." — *John 8:32.*

"Herein is our love made perfect, that we may have boldness in the day of judgment; because as he (Jesus) is, so are we in this world." — *1 John 4:17.*

Policy, Procedures & Protocols

3
Courts Of Record

The socio politico economic system we now behold is entirely flawed. Yet we support it. We complain of it to each other yet we support it, whereas, lying, stealing, and damaging other people's property is the actual problem. This information is for those who have a need to set something straight.

Setting up a Court of Record, under common law, is a practical matter rather than something to be academically studied.

Whether the issue is large or small, — to right a wrong, or to achieve justice and reparation for damage or loss, questions have to be asked and answered and faithfully recorded in a Book of Records.

Hearsay is disregarded as off public face, i.e. Hearsay is not to be written down.

So, it's unlikely to find a lawyer who will champion a cause using a Court of Record under common law where pertinent questions must be answered *"Yea, yea"* or *"Nay, nay"* *(either "Yes" or "No").*

"But let your communication be, Yea, yea; Nay, nay: for whatsoever is more than these cometh of evil." — *Matthew 5:37.*

You must locate a Notary Public to witness for you as an interface to the currently adopted de facto system . . . or in the alternative, three Men or Women can act as Witness, instead of a public notary.

Oaths are not useful in courts of record. What you want to create is an Affidavit. (See Maxims 5 & 6 below.)

10 MAXIMS OF LAW

1. A workman is worthy of his hire.

2. All men are equal under the law.

3. In commerce truth is sovereign.

4. Truth is expressed in the form of an affidavit.

5. An unrebutted affidavit stands as truth in commerce.

6. An unrebutted affidavit becomes judgement in commerce.

7. A matter must be expressed to be resolved.

8. He who leaves the field of battle first loses by default.

9. Sacrifice is the measure of credibility

10. A lien or claim can be satisfied only through rebuttal by counter affidavit point by point, resolution by jury, or payment or performance of the claim.

In the end we do it all ourselves. No lawyers are needed. Only strictly relevant, proven facts are written down on the Record. What is right and what is wrong about a particular situation.

All law is contract. Contract makes the law. **To make a contract valid, the consent of the parties must be free, mutual, and communicated.** Consent is not real or free when obtained through duress, menace, fraud, undue influence, or mistake.

The crucial and incurable flaw in all contracts is the absence of **full disclosure** and a true **meeting of the minds**, and **mutual good faith**. This absence constitutes fraud.

In order for a contract to be valid it must be entered into with **full disclosure**, **good faith** and **clean hands**.

Are the **"deliverables"** clearly and accurately specified for both parties to the contract?

Can you define the **"deliverable",** the "medium of exchange"? In other words, what is the underlying *consideration* for the contract? How does the "deliverable" come into existence?

What is the United States dollar, or a Great Britain Pound? or a Euro? If you cannot define it and explain how that "deliverable" comes into existence, how can there be a **meeting of the minds** regarding the contract?

Did one of the parties have the ability to overcome the physical limitations of nature? This is called the *"running of limitations"* which is fraud.

For example, was the substance adulterated? Were material facts withheld? Was there a misrepresentation regarding the nature of the "deliverable"?

There is no statute of limitations for fraud.

What is our right or need to know?

Surely those with offices in the Houses of Congress must

be the authority. They appear to claim that they are our representatives. Are they? Have they seen to it that the *money bills* they pass, which have been passed, are about lawful money?

Have they safeguarded our right to discharge debts at law with legitimate consideration? That is, in deliverable, verifiable, tangible substance? By neglecting this duty have they not committed **high treason** against those whom they claim to represent?

Are we not on a par with a schoolboy by comparison? At common law all men and women are truly equal. None have the right to defraud one another. They have a right to do with and on their property as they see fit. A schoolboy has a right to ask these questions equally. A cat may look at a king.

It is my right to know the facts of my life. So I must put my desire to know on **public record** by creating a **deed**, as outlined by the Magna Carta, which is the foundation of common law in many parts of the world.

There is a requirement to honorably inform other persons and parties affected by the outcome or by the process itself.

Such a **public notice** is now being given and is in the process of being served.

A true Court of Record is a superior court to any other form of court. It has original jurisdiction to determine right and wrong. From the highest viewpoint it is the **establishment of Truth** in a matter or wrongdoing.

In practical terms, the men and women of the tribunal — or the public notary if used — determine what is the just outcome of a given problem. In a Court of Record, the tribunal is independent of the magistrate.

A signature is a mark of identity and intent. With today's technology almost any mark can be forged. The solution is the Thumbprint Seal to establish a strong provable mark of identity and intent.

Common law underpins the Court of Record.

The beauty of the common law process is that it is self-correcting.

Common law is led by the requirement to find the truth appertaining to the crime and applicable to the situation.

It is not the other way around as in legal law which has multifarious boxes into which every situation is forced to fit.

Common law used to be taught at Law school. There are many people who appear to be teaching common law, but common law is not in active practice by the men and women on land. If you do not pay with *deliverable substance* for service at the clerk of a court, you are not in a Court of Record.

Courts of Record should not rush to come to conclusions regarding the Informational War that is going on in the world today.

Policy, Procedures & Protocols

4
The Hierarchy Of Law

1. Natural Law

The first order of law on this planet is **Natural Law.** Universal Principle which so necessarily agrees with nature and the state of man, that without observing their inherent maxims, the peace and happiness of society can not be preserved. Knowledge of natural law may be attained merely by the light of reason, from the facts of their essential agreeableness with the constitution of human nature. Natural Law exists regardless of whether it is enacted positively or not.

2. Commercial Law

The second order of law on this planet is **Commercial Law:** the Law of Commerce.

This most fundamental law of all human law has to do with the universal Principle of Survival. It has to do with human interactions of any kind, any relationship, buying, selling or trading; or relating to others in any way.

Commercail Law based upon treating or dealing with others in the way that you would like to be dealt with, or treated, called **The Golden Rule**.

Commercial Law has been in operation since mankind interacted with each other, begining thousands of years ago in the Sumerian/Babylonian era, where it was codified and enforced.

Ancient artifacts dating more than 6,000 years old reveal that the system was so complex at that time, it even included receipts, coined money, shopping lists, manifestos, and a postal system with the medium in baked clay.

3. Common Law

The third order of law on this planet is **Common Law,** a derivative of Commercial law and therefore the lesser of the two. Common Law (*common; co = together + munis = service, gift; exchange; to exchange together*).

Common Law emerged in England out of disputes over portions of the earth held in *allodium* (*sovereign ownership of land*) and was **based on common sense.**
Common law is the law of the land.

Common law gave rise to the jury system and the many writs and processes which governments absorbed, and statutized into rules and regulations and the regulatory procedures of the courts.

The procedures of Common Law are based on the necessity **to face your accuser - the alleged injured party - in front of witnesses,** to sort out and resolve the problem directly face to face.

Common Law was never intended to include the **construance of law** by lawyers, attorneys or judges **construing their own law,** since their Titles of Nobility are all based upon the fictions of **hear-say-evidence** which can never be the real thing.

4. Regulatory Law

The fourth order of law on the planet is **Regulatory Law.** The legal (*legislated*) Regulations of the organic republic States.

The only Law that the *States* could create was that law

which would *allow commerce to flow more efficiently WITHIN the State.*

The only Law that the *Central government, the united States of America,* could create was that law which would *allow commerce to flow more efficiently BETWEEN the States.*

Legislated regulations were never intended to regulate *the people – the "soverans."*

5. Political Law

The fifth order of law is the copyrighted, *private policy of foreign corporations,* such as **THE UNITED STATES, THE STATE OF… , THE COUNTY OF… , THE CITY OF… , etc.,** *or in other words,* POLITICS.

The purpose of these **municipalities** (*'munus,' service, gift, exchange* + *'capere' to take = to take service and exchange*) is **to govern fictitious corporate entities** such as K-MART, WAL-MART; and JOHN DOE and JANE DOE, or JACK SMITH – **not to regulate real people.**

Remember back when you thought that YOU were JOHN DOE — because that's how it is written on your drivers license?

One of our many problems — when we engage with government and other such fictional elements, in our dealings in the law — is that we have been *conditioned by public education* to interact *on **their** level,* not ours.

Never have we arisen to the level of the reality, the power, the solidity and *the pre-eminence* of the **"soveran"** that we are.

But now we can function at our level of power.

This is CHECK-MATE. The end of the Game. This is REMEDY.

Commercial Law

The principles, maxims and precepts of **Commercial Law** are the same yesterday, today, and forever. They are unchanging, unchangeable, and eternal. They are expressed in both the Old and New Testaments of the Bible.

Commercial Law, unchanged for thousands of years, is the **underlying basis of all law** on this planet and for governments around the world.

Commercial Law is the **Law of Nations** and of everything upon which human civilization is built. This is why it is so powerful.

When you operate at this level, by these precepts, nothing that is of inferior statute can overturn or change it, or abrogate it, or meddle with it. It remains the fundamental source of authority and power, and functional reality.

The Affidavit

Commerce in everyday life is the vehicle, or glue, that holds, or binds, the corporate body-politic together.

Commerce consists of a mode of interacting, doing business with, or **resolving disputes,** by which all matters are executed under oath, certified on each party's *unlimited (commercial) liability,* by sworn affidavit — *or that which is intended to possess the same effect* — as true, correct, and complete, *and not misleading* — the truth, the whole truth, and nothing but the truth.

Such an **Affidavit** is the *application* for a driver's license, or for a bank account, or to vote, or a Notary's "Certification of Copy" form, certifying a document, and a *signature* on nearly every document that the system requires citizens to be obligated to or bound.

Such *means of your signature* is an oath, or *commercial affidavit, executed under penalty of perjury,* to be *true, correct, and complete.*

In a court setting, *oral testimony* is stated in judicial terms as *orally sworn* to be *"the truth, the whole truth, and nothing but the truth, so help me God."*

In addition to asserting all matters under the solemn oath of unlimited personal, commercial, financial, and legal liability for the validity of each and every statement, the participant must provide *material evidence,* i.e. ledgering or bookkeeping *records* proving the truth, validity, relevance, and verifiability of each and every particular assertion, *to sustain credibility.*

Commerce exists and functions without respect to legal system or courts.

Policy, Procedures & Protocols

5
Maxims Of Law

There are essentially **ten maxims** of commercial law.

1. The workman is worth of his hire. — *Exodus 20:15; Lev. 19:13; Mat. 10:10; Luke 10:7; II Tim. 2:6.*

Legal maxim: *"It is against equity for the free man not to have the free disposal of his own property."*

2. All are equal under the law — "equality before the law" — *God's Law; Moral and Natural Law.* — *Exodus 21:23-25; Lev. 24: 17-21; Deut. 1;17, 19:21; Mat. 22:36-40; Luke 10:17; Col. 3:25.*

Legal maxim: *"No one is above the law."*

This maxim is founded on both natural and moral law, and is binding on everyone. For someone to say or act as though he is "above the law" is insane. This is the *major insanity in the world* today.

Man continues to live, act, believe in, and form systems, organizations, governments, laws and processes which *presume to supercede or abrogate* natural or moral law.

But, under commercial law, natural and moral law are binding on everyone, and no one can escape commercial law. Commerce, by the law of nations, ought to be common, and not converted into a monopoly for the private gain of the few.

3. In commerce truth is soverign. — *Exodus 20:16; Ps. 117:2; John 8:32; II Cor. 13:8.*

Legal maxim: *"To lie is to go against the mind."*

This Maxim is one of the most comforting Maxims we could have; our foundation for peace of mind and security and our capacity to win, and triumph — to get our Remedy in the "business" called life.

Truth is sovereign — and the "soveran" tells only the truth. ***"My word is my bond."***

If truth were *not* sovereign in commerce, *in all human action and interrelations,* there would be *no basis* for anything. No basis for law and order. No basis = no accountability. No standards. No capacity to resolve anything. It would mean that **"anything goes"** - **"each man for himself"** - **"nothing matters"** - that is *worse* than the law of the jungle.

4. Truth is expressed in the form of an Affidavit. — *Lev. 5:4-5; Lev. 6:3-5; Lev. 19:11-13: Num. 30:2; Mat. 5:33; James 5:12.*

Legal maxim: *"An affidavit is a two edged sword; that cuts both ways."*

An affidavit is your solemn expression of truth. In commerce, an affidavit must underlay and be the foundation of any commercial transaction whatsoever. There can be no valid commercial transaction without someone putting his neck on the line and stating, *"this is true, correct, complete, not meant to mislead."*

Someone has to take responsibility for saying that it is a real situation. It can be called a **True Bill** as they say in the Grand Jury.

When you **issue an affidavit** in commerce you get the **power of an affidavit.**

You *also* incur the *liability of the affidavit,* because an affidavit presents a situation where other people might be adversely affected by what you say. Things *change* by your affidavit, *which affect people's lives.*

If what you say in your affidavit is in fact *not true,* then those who are adversely affected can come back at you with *justifiable recourse* because you lied. You have told a lie *as if it were the truth.* People depend on your affidavit and they suffer loss when you lie.

5. An unrebutted affidavit stands as truth in commerce. — *12 Pet. 1:25; Heb. 6:13-15.*

Legal Maxim: *"He who does not deny, admits."*

Claims made in your affidavit, *if not rebutted point for point,* emerge as truth in Commerce.

6. An unrebutted affidavit becomes judgment in commerce. — *Heb. 6:16-17.*

There is nothing left to resolve. Any proceeding in a court, tribunal, or arbitration forum, consists of a contest (*a pistolless duel*) of commercial affidavits wherein the points that remain unrebutted in the end, **stand as truth,** as material facts from which lawful judgment is derived.

7. For any matter to be resolved it must be expressed. — *Heb. 4:16; Phil. 4:6; Eph. 6:19-21.*

Legal Maxim: *"He who fails to assert his rights has none."*

No one is expected to be a mind reader. You must put your position out there. You must state what the issue is, to have some issue to talk about, and resolve.

8. He who leaves the field of battle first loses by defaul.

Legal Maxim: *"He who does not repel a wrong, if and when he can, occasions it."*

The primary users of Commercial law, and those who best understand and codified it in Western Civilization, are the Jews. This is the *Mosaic Law* that they have relied upon for more than 3,500 years, and is based upon Babylonian Commerce. — *Book of Job; Mat. 10:22.*

An affidavit that remains unrebutted, point for point, stands as "truth in commerce" because it has not been rebutted and the contender has left the battlefield.

Governments *allegedly* exist to resolve disputes and confirm the truth; to be s*ubstitutes for the dueling field* and the *battle field* of such disputes. Conflicts of **affidavits of truth** are resolved *peaceably* and *reasonably* instead of by *violence.* People can take their unresolved disputes into court and have them opened up and resolved, instead of *going out, marching ten paces, and turning about to injure or kill.*

9. Sacrifice is the measure of credibility. — "Nothing ventured nothing gained."

Legal Maxim: *"He who bears the burden ought to derive the benefit".*

NO WILLINGNESS TO SACRIFICE SHOWS NO LIABILITY, RESPONSIBILITY, AUTHORITY OR MEASURE OF CONVICTION.

A person must **put himself on the line** and assume a position, **take a stand,** regarding the matter at hand.

One cannot realize *a potential gain* without exposing himself to *a potential loss.* One who is not willing to swear an oath, on his unlimited commercial liability, and claim authority for the truth of his statements, and legitimacy of his actions, has no basis to assert his claims or charges, and forfeits all credibility and right. (*Acts 7, life/ death of Stephen*).

10. <u>A claim or lien can be staisfied only by rebuttable affidavit point by point, resolution by jury, or payment of the claim</u>. — *Genesis 2:3; Matthew IV; Revelation.*

Legal Maxim: *"Prove your case, or the accused is absolved"*.

In commerce, a lien or claim can only be satisfied in any **one** of the following **three ways** . . .

10.1. ...by someone rebutting your affidavit with an affidavit of his own, point by point, until the matter is resolved as to *whose claims* are correct.

10.2. ...convene a common-law jury concerning a dispute involving a claim of more than $20.00 based on the Seventh Amendment to the Constitution, or use a tribunal of three disinterested parties to confirm judgment.

10.3. ...pay the claim.

6
Definitions

The two building blocks that must be structured in order for the Republic for the united States of America to be solidly grounded to secure our liberties are 1) a **Law forum** and 2) a **free hold of the Land.**

Out of these two fundamental structures will emerge the basis for building a sound monetary and economic structure that will rebuild America on a national level and provide the strength to secure our international relationships with the world.

The main building block in a Republic is the **Soveran;** the individual who declares his or her sovereign rights and enters into a social political compact to retain, preserve, and protect the fundamentals of his or her rights, land, family and life, by establishing a **Jural Assembly** with other soverans of his peers at the local level.

The lawful authority of the **local** (county) **assembly** becomes the building block of the sovereign state republic, and the sovereign state republic then enters, on an equal footing, the national union of republics which form the **Republic for the united States of America.**

Soveran: The sovereign individual is a living man or woman who is not bonded as a surety against a system of perpetual debt, who walks, talks and breaths free on the land, who declares, holds, and retains unalienable sovereign rights to live life free by the guidance of their own free moral agency and conscience, without external dictates as long as they honor and respect the same in others and do not cause injury in any way.

Common law: Common law is the basis of commonly accepted, locally organized principles of jurisprudence by which people, in local assembly, organize their law forum (forum of law) for the management and settlement of issues and disputes that arise from time to time from living together in a free society.

If there is no injured party or breach of contract, there is no controversy, and if this be the case and/or if someone or some entity is not party to a contract, they do not have a basis of claim in the common law.

The **local forum** is established within the Republic for the united States of America by convening the Jural Assembly of men and women in the local county, and from there ratifying a county settlement constitution under which to be governed.

The **settlement constitution** establishes the basis for the claim of land of metes and bounds within the boundaries of the counties within each state republic. The **settlement constitution** also provides for the creation of office seats that are filled upon ratification of the constitution.

These seats include: Governor, Attorney General, Supreme Court Justice, Sheriff, Library of Records Archivist and Secretary, Land Records Clerk, County Treasurer, Justice of the Peace, Grand Jury Foreman, Chief Notary and Postmaster General. Other offices may be added as required from time to time.

The key to the creation of the **law forum** is the establishment of a system of records to create a permanent record of all lawful due process and to provide the ability to issue certified copies.

Each county will have a **Library of Records** for physical archiving and there will be an electronic system of records available on each county web site and the state republic web site bureau of records. Once this system is complete it will eliminate the need for using de facto recorders, many of whom use their position to block and undermine lawful processes.

The archivist is the **Custodian of Records,** a key position for a permanent system of records within a law forum. Parallel to the library of records for general county documents and for the law forum will be a system of land records, also essential as we perfect the process of bringing land under free hold into the county and the republic. Due process and equal protection in law cannot be functional until the record keeping system is in place.

Additionally, basic infrastructure and systems must be developed and put in place to handle how cases are entered into the forum, management of cases, payment of fees and other necessary functions.

After the ratification of the **county settlement constitution** and all of the infrastructure and record keeping is in place, the people of the county Jural Assembly will have come together with the superior authority that has been held by the people in North America since 1776.

By virtue of the fact of the people having reinhabited the republics of all fifty states and the national republic as well, in 2010, and having reclaimed the land and the law thereby, we now stand on the land as sovereign soverans and have established our law forum and venue for proper adjudication and enforcement thereof.

The court of the soveran is where he or she brings himself or herself into the forum to establish a court of record. The court thusly established is the court of the moving party who brings the action.

COURT: The person and suit of the sovereign; the place where the sovereign sojourns with his regal retinue, wherever that may be. (*Black's Law Dictionary, 5th edition, page 318.*) (*sojourn: a temporary stay.*)

COURT: An agency of the sovereign created by it directly or indirectly under its authority, consisting of one or more officers, established and maintained for the purpose of hearing and determining issues of law and fact regarding legal rights and alleged violations there of, and of applying the sanctions of the law, authorized to exercise its powers in the courts of law at times and places previously determined by lawful authority. (*Isbill v. Stovall, Tex.Civ.App. 92 S.W.2d 1067, 1070; Black's Law Dictionary, 4th edition, page 425.*)

Notice that this second definition states that the court is "authorized to exercise its powers in the course of law at times and places previously determined by lawful authority." This is exactly the definition of our law forum.

The people in the republic retain and exercise their lawful authority. By such authority, we establish our county structure of self-governance from which the law forum has been created to provide a time and place (venue) into which the soveran may sojourn in order to set up his or her court.

The soveran places his or her moving document (action)

into the law forum, establishes the venue "in the course of law" by providing a time and a place where the court can proceed in its business, all of which has previously been determined by the lawful authority of the people.

The courts of the people are Courts of Record, hence the necessity for the system of records, office holders and structure as previously described.

The moving document (complaint) of the soveran establishes his or her evidence to establish the record. The authority of the court and the law forum of the county will then issue a summons for the named defendants to appear into the law forum to defend against the action brought against them (the complaint).

The defendants must appear in their natural person, not through an attorney, although they may choose and have any counsel they wish. They are not to bring limited liability bonding or protection afforded corporate entities or their officers within the corporate public jurisdiction in a court of common law.

They must answer the complaint in their own status and capacities. If they do not appear by answering the complaint, they have the right to a trial by jury because the jury is there to protect the rights of the accused.

Since the court is the court of the soveran who brought the initial action (the complaint) and who can also establish the law of the case, the jury has the authority to determine both the issues of fact and the law.

If the law upon which the action has been brought is just and the facts sustain the complaint, then the issues will be settled most likely in favor of the moving party. If the law is not just, then the jury can nullify any decision or judgment brought by the court.

In addition to the fact that all defendants must appear as living men and women without limited liability, there are no codes or statutes allowed in a court of law, thus eliminating the vast amount of obfuscation, distortion and manipulation existent today in the administrative tribunal that most of the public believe are courts of law, which they emphatically are not.

COURT OF RECORD: To be a Court of Record a court must have four characteristics, and may have a fifth. A Court of Record must have . . .

1. ...a judicial tribunal having attributes and exercising functions independently of the person of the magistrate designated generally to hold it.
2. ...proceedings according to the course of common law.
3. ...acts and judicial proceedings recorded for a perpetual memory and testimony.
4. ...the power to fine or imprison for contempt.
5. ...generally a seal (optional).
Black's Law Dictionary, 4th edition, pp. 425, 426.

Once the action has been entered and the court established, the tribunal (court/sovereign) has the authority to issue writs and orders.

A writ of injunction (order to cease and desist) or writ of mandamus (order to comply) can be issued, for example, to an inferior jurisdiction to stop any proceeding (i.e., suit of unlawful detainer or foreclosure) that is moving against something now brought within the jurisdiction of the superior court (our lawful Courts of Record) by a writ of removal.

The obvious example is a property under attack by the machinations of the de facto system through foreclosure or otherwise.

Keep in mind that "property" refers to what is attached to the equity (corporate/de facto system); land is what belongs in and never left the lawful Republic and can be brought back by making the claim of right that will be later further discussed.

The first characteristic in the above list states that the tribunal exercises functions independent of the magistrate. This means that the soveran is the tribunal because he or she established his or her Court of Record and it proceeds according to the common law.

The Magistrate or judge does not have judicial authority, only ministerial authority to administer and in effect referee the case and process.

This also applies to when an individual properly brings an action in law into the de facto court system, but of course the judges there do not like being relegated to ministerial functions, so they usually attempt to trick the soveran into releasing his or her court and traversing back into equity where the judge controls.

This problem will be eliminated once we have our functioning law forum in place in the counties of the republics. The issue, of course, is ultimately a question of enforcement, which will be addressed at a later time.

Setting aside that point for the moment, the point to understand is that the law forum, as described, is established to create the **venue** into which we as the soverans may sojourn to establish our courts of record.

We are the court, not a place or a building. We retain our regal retinue and bring it into our courts.

Our system of permanent record keeping is a part of the soveran's regal retinue, because originally the courtiers were there for the pleasure of the king to retain the permanent record of proceedings; no our physical and electronic records will serve that purpose.

All of this describes the non-criminal side of the law forum.

Once the action and case has been settled by a judgment order, and that order is issued such as for example to quiet title claims of all other parties to property or land, if any such orders are not complied with then this becomes the evidence to be brought before the Grand Jury for consideration.

An order for quiet title issued by a settled case, writs of mandamus, prohibition, removal, injunction or otherwise might be issued by our proper law forum and directed towards a de facto court, judge, magistrate, police officer, sheriff or other de facto actors or officers, and if not complied with, such non-compliance becomes the evidence of criminal trespass on such lawful orders, warranting being brought by criminal complaint and charge before the Grand Jury.

The de jure Grand Jury is the highest form of law and enforcement of the people.

Corpus Juris Secundum, Article 38A, Section 9 (page 340) states:

"There cannot be a Grand Jury de facto when there is a Grand Jury de jure."

Based on this simply statement, our de jure Grand Juries at the county, state and national levels effectively nullify current de facto Grand Juries.

The de jure Grand Jury is established and convened to be the forum that the people can bring charging documents and supporting evidence forward in order to have the Grand Jury review and determine whether a bill of criminal indictment should be issued.

The Grand Jury, upon review of a charging complaint and the evidence (oral testimony and documentary) is required to issue a True Bill or No Bill.

If a No Bill is issued, the case is dropped due to lack of sufficient evidence to warrant prosecution.

If a True Bill is issued, the bill is then forwarded to the free state Attorney General for issuance of indictments and initiation of prosecution.

The cases will be heard by the county supreme court or an inferior court established within the forum as may be required to handle case loads. Both the supreme court, inferior courts, courts of record established by the sovereign and the grand jury have summons and subpoena power.

Finally, the issue of enforcement must be addressed.

It is all well and good to create all of the above, to hold our courts, establish our records, build our evidence and issue our orders and writs, but if these are only toothless junk yard dogs with no bite and no enforcement we are only really just play acting and not gaining real remedy.

To be sure, at this time, there is no real answer that can be put forth as to exactly how this enforcement and remedy will become a reality.

But knowing that we have work ahead and miles to travel to get to that point does not provide us the luxury of giving up before starting, or scorning those who are working hard to make the republic and our law forums a reality.

Those who are doing so are part of the problem whereas we are about solutions.

Just because it is a hard task does not provide reason to avoid the journey, and as the saying goes, "The difficult we do today, the impossible takes a little longer."

One either sits back in his or her arm chair and becomes immobilized with the attitude of "I'll believe it when I see it," or gets off his or her butt, rolls up his or her sleeves, gets to work and knows it will become real because "I believe it, therefore I see it."

Rome wasn't built in a day, it took two thousand years, and we are living in its last dying days, so if it takes us a little while to get this in place and put teeth into the old dog to defend our lives, our land, our families, and our country, then let's stop complaining and get to work.

Be that as it may, this author sees and believes that we will persevere, and we will triumph in this goal.

Enforcement will come when critical mass is reached, when there are enough players willing to work and to take a stand, and enough counties seated and when the national republic gains further strength through current activities and events.

At such a time, enforcement will come by a combination of many things.

One is our ability to execute our enforcement through grand jury True Bills followed by indictments, summons and subpoenas that if not complied with, are followed by arrest bonds and claims upon risk management departments.

Our actions are built on the foundation of forgiveness, not for retribution or revenge, but to return lawful order to the land.

Establishing and activating the proper law forum in each

county and in each republic free state is the first building block to achieving our goals.

Lawful remedy, with enforcement, will come when we are in place and capable of performing that which needs to be done. The framework for achieving this is already in hand; all that remains is building the structure outlined.

We need experienced patriots who have studied law and understand the deeper implications of our Cause. Never before has the maxim "United we stand, Divided We Fall" been more appropriate than today.

Policy, Procedures & Protocols

7
The De Facto And The De Jure

From Black's Law Dictionary Revised 4th ed. ppg. 824, 825

GOVERNMENT DE FACTO: A government of fact. A government actually exercising power and control in the state, as opposed to the true and lawful government; a government not established according to the constitution of the state, or not lawfully entitled to recognition or supremacy, but which has nevertheless supplanted or displaced the government *de jure.* A government deemed unlawful, or deemed wrongful or unjust, which, nevertheless, receives presently habitual obedience from the bulk of the community. —Aust. Jur. 324.

There are several degrees of what is called "*de facto* government." Such a government, in its highest degree, assumes a character very closely resembling that of a lawful government. This is when the usurping government expels the regular authorities from their customary seats and function, and establishes itself in their place, and so becomes the actual government of a country. The distinguishing characteristic of such a government is that its adherents, in war against the government *de jure,* do not incur the penalties of treason; and the obligations it assumes, in behalf of the country or otherwise, will in general be respected by the government *de jure* when restored.

Such a government might be more aptly denominated a "government of paramount force," being maintained by active military power against the rightful authority of an established and lawful government; and obeyed in civil matters by private citizens. They are usually administered directly by military authority, but they may be administered, also, by civil authority, supported more or less by military force. — Thorington v. Smith, 8 Wall. 8,9,19 L.Ed.361.

GOVERNMENT DE JURE: A government of right; the true and lawful government; a government established according to the constitution of the state, and lawfully entitled to recognition and supremacy and the administration of the state, but which is actually cut off from power or control. A government deemed lawful, or deemed rightful or just, which nevertheless, has been supplanted or displaced; that is to say, which receives not presently (although it received formerly) habitual obedience from the bulk of the community. —Aust. Jur. 324.

8
The Grand Jury

In the common law, a **Grand Jury** is a type of jury that determines whether there is enough evidence for a trial.

Grand juries carry out this duty by examining evidence presented to them by a *prosecutor,* and issuing *indictments,* or by investigating *alleged crimes* and issuing *presentments.*

A *grand jury* is traditionally larger than, and distinguishable from a *petit* jury, which is used during a trial.

A grand jury is meant to be part of the system of checks and balances, preventing a case from going to trial on a prosecutor's bare word. A prosecutor must convince the grand jury, an impartial panel of ordinary citizens, that there exists *reasonable suspicion, probable cause,* or a *prima facie case* that a crime has been committed.

The grand jury can compel witnesses to testify before them. Unlike the trial itself, the grand jury's proceedings are secret; the accused and his or her counsel are generally not present for the testimony of witnesses. The grand jury's decision is either a **"True Bill"** (meaning that there is a case to answer), or **"No Bill".**

In the State of Louisiana there is a third option, **"By pretermitting entirely the matter investigated"**. This requires nine of the twelve grand jurors finding that *there is not enough evidence presented* to determine if a person should or should not be charged with a crime.

Jurors typically are drawn from the same pool of citizens as a petit jury, and participate for a specific period of time.

NOTE: The following rules only apply to a Republic such as the uSA. For a Monarchy such as Great Britain substitute the word "baron" for "people", and substitute the word "subject" for "citizen". Also, in the uSA, a peer is one of the people (not citizens). In Great Britain, a peer is one of the nobility.

Common Law Grand Jury

Rules

APPLICABLE LAW

The government must accept the Magna Carta as common law when pleaded as such.

Source: Confirmatio Cartarum, Article 1

http://www.1215.org/lawnotes/lawnotes/cartarum.htm

Basic requirements and procedures for a common law grand jury:

Source: Magna Carta, Articles 52 & 61

http://www.1215.org/lawnotes/lawnotes/magna.htm#52

http://www.1215.org/lawnotes/lawnotes/magna.htm#61

HOW CONSTITUTED

Grand jury members must be elected by the people (not citizens) of the jurisdiction in which they are operating.

There are no rules defining a procedure for how they are elected. The people, without the influence of government, decide for themselves how the grand jury members are elected.

There must be 25 members.

QUALIFICATIONS

The members must be "people" of the jurisdiction and not "citizens" of the jurisdiction.

For example, they must be "People of the united States," or "People of California," or "People of the State of California"; not "citizen of the United States," nor "citizen of California," nor "citizen of the State of California."

http://www.1215.org/lawnotes/lawnotes/pvc.htm
http://www.1215.org/lawnotes/lawnotes/sovreign.htm

Each member must be sworn in and promise to observe all of these rules and, so far as within his power, cause all the rules to be observed.

QUORUM

When the grand jury meets, if any are absent after being summoned, then those present constitute a quorum.

All decisions of the grand jury are decided by majority vote of members present.

If any member dies or leaves the country, or in any other way is prevented from carrying out the grand jury's decisions, the remaining grand jurors shall choose another to fill his place and he shall likewise be sworn in.

FINALITY OF DECISIONS

No decision of a grand jury is reviewable in any court of the government.

JURISDICTION

Any government transgression against anyone in any respect.

Any government breaking articles of peace or security.

Any dispute regarding anyone who has been disseized or removed, by the government, without a legal sentence of his peers, from his lands, castles, liberties or lawful right.

Procedure I
DISPUTE SETTLEMENT

If the grand jury is informed of any dispute regarding anyone who has been disseized or removed, by the government without a legal sentence of his peers, from his lands, castles, liberties or lawful right, then the dispute shall be settled by the grand jury.

Procedure II
ENFORCEMENT

Four of the members must be shown that because of the government . . .

A. ...a transgression has occurred against any one in any respect, or

B. ...some one of the articles of peace or security has been broken

The four members must show to the government the government's error.

The four members must ask the government to amend that error without delay. If the government does not amend the error within 40 days after being shown the error, then the four members shall refer the matter to the remainder of the grand jury.

The grand jury may distrain and oppress the government in every way in their power, namely, by taking the homes, lands, possessions, and any way else they can until amends shall have been made according to the sole judgment of the grand jury.

LIMITATION OF POWERS

The grand jury may not imprison or execute any government personnel or their children.

PUBLIC SUPPORT

Anyone (people or citizen) who chooses to help enforce the grand jury decision must first swear that he will obey the mandates of the grand jury, and that with them to the extent of his power he will impose the grand jury's decisions upon the government.

The authority to support the grand jury is pre-authorized by the government.

If anyone refuses to support a grand jury decision, the government will force him to swear his support of the grand jury.

LIMITATIONS ON GOVERNMENT

The government is prohibited from doing anything to diminish the effect of the grand jury.

If the government does prohibit or diminish the effectiveness of the grand jury, it shall be vain and invalid and may not be used in any later proceeding by the government or anyone else.

TERMINATION OF ENFORCEMENT

When all issues are settled to the satisfaction of the grand jury, things shall return to normal as they were before. No grudges.

9

Reactivating
The Common Law Grand Jury

BACKGROUND

When the colonies separated from England, King George retaliated by revoking their charters. Technically, the colonies were without any legal authority to operate.

However, civics (the branch of political philosophy concerned with individual rights) was generally taught and known by the people who asserted their rights and maintained order by applying the common law. The people united in the form of common law grand juries and continued the functioning of government.

As the legislatures matured they slowly increased governmental power while simultaneously reducing personal sovereign power. This was done through a combination of passing pro-government legislation and reducing or eliminating education about civics. Today, two and a quarter centuries later, hardly anyone even knows the meaning of the word, "civics."

Despite the fact that the state and federal constitutions still acknowledge the common law as the ultimate law system, people everywhere are falsely conditioned to believe that statutory law and codes are the only source of law.

The only remaining generally known common law term among the public is "common law marriage."

The common law grand jury is now dormant only because of public ignorance of its powers that supercede all other government entities, including the modern statutorily defined grand jury.

Awakening the grand jury will not be graciously accepted by the government. A strategy is needed to reintroduce this fundamental protection against injustice and tyranny.

STEP 1
ESTABLISH LEGITIMACY

The first step is to get public acceptance. Every dictator in history understands the power of the people and cultivates their support either through enticements or threats.

Reactivating the grand jury concept will go through four traditional stages: ***denial, ridicule, violent opposition,*** then ***self-evident acceptance.***

Theoretically, the grand jury can meet anywhere, anytime. But that is hardly a good image. One way to get public acceptance, and minimize denial, ridicule, and violent opposition, is to hold the grand jury sessions in the public court house.

The foreman could apply to a court administrator for use of one of the rooms in the public courthouse. If it is refused, then the court administrator should, under common law procedures, be sued for his dereliction of duty.

The grand jury should follow normal protocol.

In other words, if the *grand jury* begins a process on its own, the resulting accusation is called a *presentment.*

If a *prosecutor* originates a process, the jury returns to the prosecutor an *indictment* on acceptance (also called a *"true bill"*), or a *"no bill"* on denial.

[Note: be careful with your words. Wrong words may result in inaction! If you call the *presentment* an *indictment,* the prosecutor may feel no obligation because he did not initiate the process!]

STEP 2
GAIN PUBLIC ACCEPTANCE

The second step is to start small. The grand jury could take on issues which anyone can easily see should be prosecuted. As public acceptance increases, the grand jury can enlarge its field of inquiry. The grand jury should have a strong public relations program for this step.

STEP 3
TAKE ON LARGER PROJECTS

The third step is to take on grander objectives. If the first two steps are well executed, then this step will be the easiest. With both legitimacy and acceptance established the grand jury can make itself felt.

dis·sei**z**e or dis·sei**s**e: *tr.v.* dis·seized or dis·seised, dis·seiz·ing or dis·seis·ing, dis·seiz·es or dis·seis·es. *Law:* **To dispossess unlawfully of real property; to oust.**

dis·seize: *–verb (used with object),* -seized, -seiz·ing. *Law:* **To deprive** (a person) **of seizin, or of the possession, of a freehold interest in land, esp. wrongfully or by force; to oust.**

Policy, Procedures & Protocols

10
Common Law

Common Law is the common sense rooted in the Bible. In 1776 we came out of bondage against great odds to achieve Liberty. Liberty is that delecate area between the force of government and man's free will. Liberty brings freedom of choice; to work, to trade, to go, and to live wherever one wishes.

Liberty leads to Abundance. Abundance results in Complacency. Complacency leads to Apathy. Apathy brings Dependency, where dependents are not aware that they are dependent; they delude themselves by thinking that they are still free. Then Dependency becomes Bondage.

There are a few ways out of bondage. Bloodshed and war often result, but our founding fathers found a better way.

Realizing that the Creator is always above that which He creates, they established a three way system by which an informed People properly can manage those who act in the name of government.

To be a good steward of God's government one must understand the chain of command in the Republic:

1. God created man.
2. Man created Constitutions.
3. Constitutions created government.
4. Government created corporations, etc.

The higher power is supposed to remain in the People, but it was lost to those leaders acting in the name of government: politicians, bureaucrats, judges, lawyers, etc.

As a result America began to function as a democracy instead of a Republic. A democracy is dangerous because it is a one-choice system as opposed to a Republic, which is a three-choice system: three choices to check tyranny, not just one.

Our first choice is when we choose those who are to represent us in the seats of government. But the People have not been educated about the other two choices.

Our other two choices are the most effective means by which the people of any nation on earth have had of controlling those appointed to serve them in government.

The second choice you have comes when you serve on a Grand Jury. Before anyone can be brought to trial for an infamous or capital crime by those acting in the name of government, your permission must be obtained. Permission must be obtained from the people serving on the Grand Jury!

A Grand Jury's purpose is to protect the public from an overzealous prosecution.

The third choice is when you are acting as a jury member during a courtroom trial. In this setting each Juror has more power than the President, all of Congress, and all of the judges combined!

Congress can make laws (legislate), the President or some other bureaucrat can give orders or issue regulations, and judges may instruct, or make a decisions, but no Juror can be punished for choosing to vote "Not Guilty!" Any Juror can choose to disregard the instructions of any judge or attorney in rendering his vote.

If only one Juror should vote "Not Guilty" for any reason, there is no conviction and no punishment at the end of the trial. Those acting in the name of government must come to the common man to get his *permission* to enforce a law!

As a Juror in a trial setting, when it comes to your individual choice of innocent or guilty, you are answerable alone only to almighty God.

The First Amendment to the Constitution was born out of this great concept. However, most judges today refuse to inform Jurors of their rights.

At the time of the adoption of the Constitution, the jury's role, as defense against political oppression, was unquestioned in American jurisprudence. This Republic survived until the 1850's, before which prosecutions under the Fugitive Slave Act were largely unsuccessful because juries refused to convict the accused.

Then judges began to erode the institution of free juries, leading to the **absurd compromise** that is the current state of the law. While our courts uniformly hold that juries have the power to return a verdict of not guilty whatever the facts, they routinely tell the jurors just the opposite.

Further, the courts will not allow the defendants or their counsel to inform the jurors of their true jural power. A lawyer who would do this would face professional discipline and charges of contempt of court.

By what logic should juries have the power to acquit a defendant but not have the right to know about this power called jury nullification?

More than logic has suffered. As originally conceived, juries were to be a safety valve, a way to soften the rigidity of the judicial system by introducing the community's common sense. If they are to function effectively as the "conscience of the community", jurors must be told that they have the power to say "No" to a prosecution in order to achieve a greater good. To cut jurors off from this information is to undermine one of our most important institutions; that of trial by jury itself.

The community should educate itself. Then citizens called for jury duty could teach the judges a needed lesson in civics.

Grand Juries and *Petit Juries* are designed to bring to light a very important institution our nation's founders provided to insure that the People rule this nation, instead of the growing tyranny of politicians, judges, lawyers, and bureaucrats.

This book focuses on the true power you possess as a Juror, how you got it, why you have it, and remind you of the foundation on which you must decide, not only the facts placed in evidence before you, but also the validity of every law, rule, regulation, ordinance, or instruction given by any man seated as a judge or attorney, when you serve as a Juror.

One Juror can stop tyranny with a "Not Guilty" vote! He can nullify bad law in any case, by "hanging" the jury!

"I am only one, but I am one. I cannot do everything, but I can do something. What I can do, I should do and, with the help of God, I will do!" — Everett Hale

The only power the judge has over the jury is their ignorance! We must relearn a desperately needed lesson in civics. The truth of this has been answered by many testimonies and historical events.Consider the following:

11
Jury Rights

"The jury has a right to judge both the law as well as the fact in controversy." — John Jay, 1st Chief Justice U.S. supreme Court (1789).

"The jury has the right to determine both the law and the facts." — Samuel Chase, U.S. Supreme Court Justice. 1796, Signer of The unanimous Declaration.

"The jury has the power to bring a verdict in the teeth of both law and fact." — Oliver Wendell Holmes, U.S. Supreme Court Justice (1902).

"The law itself is on trial quite as much as the cause which is to be decided." — Harlan F. Stone, 12th Chief Justice U.S. Supreme Court (1941).

"The pages of history shine on instances of the jury's exercise of its prerogative to disregard instructions of the judge . . ." — U.S. vs. Dougheny, 473 F 2nd 1113, 1139 (1972).

12
The Law Of The Land

The general misconception is that any statute passed by legislators bearing the **appearance** of law constitutes the law of the land.

The U. S. Constitution is the supreme law of the land, and any statute, to be valid, must be in agreement with it.

It is impossible for a law which violates the Constitution to be valid. This is succinctly stated as follows:

"All laws which are repugnant to the Constitution are null and void." — Marbury vs. Madison, 5 US (2 Cranch) 137, 174, 176 (1803).

"Where rights secured by the Constitution are involved, there can be no rule making or legislation which would abrogate them." — Miranda vs. Arizona, 384 US 436 p. 491.

"An unconstitutional act is not law; it confers no rights; it imposes no duties; affords no protection; it creates no office; it is in legal contemplation, as inoperative as though it had never been passed." — Norton vs. Shelby County 118 US 425 p. 442.

The general rule is that an unconstitutional statute, though having the *form* and the *name* of law, is in reality no law, but is wholly void and ineffective for any purpose; since unconstitutionality dates from the time of its enactment, and not merely from the date of the decision so branding it.

"No one is bound to obey an unconstitutional law and no courts are bound to enforce it." — 16 Am Jur 2d, See 177 late 2d, See 256.

13
The Ten Commandments

The Ten Commandments represent God's government over man! God commands us for our own good to give up wrongs and not rights! His system results in Freedom and Liberty!

The Constitution and the Bill of Rights are built on this foundation, which provides for punitive justice. It is not until one damages another's person or property that a man can be punished.

God's system leads to Liberty; the Marxist system leads to bondage. Read carefully:

1. Thou shalt have no other gods before Me.
2. Thou shalt not make unto thee any graven image.
3. Thou shall not take the name of the Lord thy God in vain.
4. Remember the Sabbath to keep it holy.
5. Honor thy father and mother.
6. Thou shalt not murder.
7. Thou shalt not commit adultery.
8. Thou shall not steal.
9. Thou shall not bear false witness.
10. Thou shalt not covet

Directly above the Chief Justice's Chair is a tablet signifying the Ten Commandments. When the Speaker of the House in the U.S. Congress looks up, his eyes look into the face of Moses. *"The Bible is the Book upon which this Republic rests."* — Andrew Jackson, Seventh President of the United States.

"The moral principles and precepts contained in the Scriptures ought to form the basis of all our civil constitutions and laws. All the miseries and evils which men suffer from, vice, crime, ambition, injustice, oppression, slavery, and war, proceed from their despising or neglecting the precepts contained in the Bible." — Noah Webster.

14
The Communist Manifesto

The Communist Manifesto represents a misguided philosophy which teaches the citizens to give up their **Rights** for the sake of the "common good" but this philosopy always ends in a police state. This philosophy is called preventive justice. Control is the key concept. Read carefully:

1. Abolition of private property.
2. Heavy progressive income tax.
3. Abolition of all rights of inheritance.
4. Confiscation of property of all emigrants and rebels.
5. Central bank.
6. Government control of Communications and Transportation.
7. Government ownership of factories and agriculture.
8. Government control of labor.
9. Corporate farms, regional planning.
10. Government control of education.

GIVE UP RIGHTS FOR THE "COMMON GOOD"?

Where the people fear the government you have tyranny where the government fears the people, you have liberty.

Politicians, bureaucrats, and especially judges, would have you believe that too much freedom will result in chaos. So we should gladly give up some of our **Rights** "for the good of the community."

In other words, people acting in the name of government, say we need more laws, and more Officers to enforce these laws, even if we have to give up some **Rights** in the process.

They believ that the more laws we have, the more control we have, thus a better society. This theory may sound good on paper, and apparently many of our leaders think this way, as evidenced by the thousands of new laws that are added to the books each year in this country. But no matter how this Marxist argument is made, the fact is that whenever you give up a **Right** you lose a **free Choice**!

The real name of control is **Bondage.** If giving up some **Rights** produces a better society, then by giving up All of our **Rights** we could produce a perfect society. We could chain everybody to a tree; for lack of **Trust.**

This might prevent crime, but it would destroy **Privacy**, which is the heartbeat of **Freedom!** It would destroy **Trust,** the foundation of **Dignity.** Instead of giving up **RIGHTS,** we should give up **wrongs**.

The opposite of control is not chaos. More laws do not make for less crime. We must give up wrongs, not rights, for a better society.

"Necessity is the plea for every infringement of human liberty; it is the argument of tyrants; it is the creed of slaves." — William Pitt, of the British House of Commons.

15
Inalienable Natural Rights

Natural Rights are those rights such as Life; Liberty; and the Pursuit of Happiness. Freedom of Religion; Speech; Learning; Travel; Self-Defense; etc.

Laws and statutes which violate Natural Rights are not law but impostors. The U.S. Constitution was written to protect our Natural Rights from being tampered with by legislators.

Our forefathers knew that the U.S. Constitution would be worthless to restrain government legislators unless it was clearly understood that the people had the right to compel the government to keep within Constitutional bounds.

In a jury trial the real judges are the Jurors. Judges are actually Referees bound by the Constitution.

Government is established to protect the weak from the strong. This is the purpose for establishing all legitimate government.

Only the weaker party lose their liberties when a government becomes oppressive. The stronger party are free by virtue of their superior strength. They never oppress themselves.

Legislation is the work of the stronger party.

If the stronger party have the sole power of determining what legislation shall be enforced, they have all power in their hands, and the weaker party are subjects of a government that is absolute.

Unless the weaker party have a veto, they have no power whatever in the government ... no liberties.

The trial by jury is the only institution that gives the weaker party a veto of the power of the stronger.

Trial by jury is the only institution that gives the weaker party a voice in the government or any guaranty against oppression.

16
Jury Tampering

A JURY'S Rights, Powers and Duties:
The Charge to the Jury in the first Jury Trial before the Supreme Court of the United States illustrates the true power of the Jury. In the February term of 1794, the Supreme Court conducted a Jury trial and said:

"It is presumed, that the juries are the best judges of facts; on the other hand, it is presumed that the courts are the best judges of law. But still, both objects are within your power of decision. You have a right to take upon yourselves ***to judge of both, to determine the law as well as the fact in controversy."*** — State of Georgia vs. Brailsford, et al, 3 Dall. I.

"The Jury has an unreviewable and unreversible power to acquit in disregard of the instructions on the law given by trial judge ..." — U.S. vs. Dougherty, 473 F 2nd 1113, 1139 (1972).

Hence Jury disregard of the conviction-oriented evidence presented for its consideration, and Jury disregard for what the trial judge wants them to believe, is the controlling law in any particular case. "Jury lawlessness" (*willingness to nullify bad law*) is not to be avoided, but rather encouraged.

"Jury lawlessness is the greatest corrective of law in its actual administration. The will of the state at large imposed on a reluctant community, the will of a majority imposed on a vigorous and determined minority, find the same obstacle in the local Jury that formerly confronted kings and ministers." — U.S. vs. Dougherty, 473 F 2nd 1113, 1139 (1972).

17
Right Of The Jury To Be Told

Almost every Jury in the land is falsely instructed by the judge that it must accept as law that which is given to them by the court, and that the Jury can decide only the facts of the case. This destroys the purpose of the Common Law Jury, and permits the imposition of tyranny upon a people

"There is nothing 'more terrifying than ignorance in action." — Goethe (engraved on a plaque at the Naval War College).

"To embarrass justice by a multiplicity of law, or to hazard justice by confidence in judges, are the rocks on which all civil institutions have been wrecked." — Johnson (engraved in Minnesota State Capitol Outside the Supreme Court Chambers).

"...the letter killeth but the spirit giveth life." — 2nd Corinthians 3:6.

"Error needs the support of government. Truth can stand by itself." — Thomas Jefferson.

The **JURY'S** options are not limited by the choices presented to it in the courtroom.

"The jury gets its understanding, as to the arrangements in the legal system, from more than one voice. There is the formal communication of the 'judge.' There is the informal communication from the total culture — literature; current comment, conversation; and, of course, history and tradition." — U.S. vs. Dougherty, 473 F 2nd 1113, 1139 (1972).

Without the power to decide what facts, law and evidence are applicable; Juries cannot be a protection to the accused.

If people acting in the name of government are permitted by Jurors to dictate any law whatever, they can also unfairly dictate what evidence is admissible or inadmissible and thereby prevent the whole truth from being considered.

Thus, if government can manipulate and control both the law and evidence, the issue of fact becomes virtually irrelevant. In reality, true Justice would be denied leaving us with a trial by government and not a trial by Jury.

18
How Tyranny Begins

Unchecked power is the foundation of tyranny.

It is the Juror's duty to use the Jury Room as a vehicle to stem the tide of tyranny and oppression: to prevent bloodshed by peacefully taking power away from those who have abused it. The Jury is the primary vehicle for the peaceable restoration of Liberty, Power, and Honor, to the People.

Your vote of Not Guility must be respected by all other members of the Jury. It is the RIGHT and the DUTY of a JUROR to never yield his or her sacred vote, for you are not there as a fool, to simply agree with the majority, but as an Officer of the Court and a qualified judge in your own right.

Regardless of the pressures or abuse that might be heaped on you by any other members of the Jury, with whom you may in good conscience disagree, you can await the reading of the verdict secure in the knowledge that you have voted your conscience, and convictions, and not those of someone else.

You are not a Rubber Stamp.

By what logic do we send our youth to battle tyranny on foreign soil, while we refuse to do so in our courts? Many of the planks of the "Communist Manifesto" are represented by law in the United States. How is it possible for Americans to denounce Communism while practice it at the same time.

The JURY judges the spirit, motive, and intent of both the law and the accused, while the prosecutor represents only the letter of the law.

Herein lies the opportunity to provide "Liberty and Justice for All." If you and numerous other Jurors throughout the nation and states bring in verdicts of "Not Guilty" in cases where a **man-made** statute is oppresive or defective, these statutes will become ineffective and void.

"If ye love wealth better than liberty, the tranquility of servitude better than the animating contest of freedom, go home from us in peace. We ask not your counsels or your arms. Crouch down and lick the hands which feed you. May your chains set lightly upon you, and may posterity forget that ye were our countrymen." — Samuel Adams.

19
Patrick Henry Stunned

Young Christian attorney Patrick Henry saw first hand why a Jury of Peers is so vital to Freedom. When in March 1775 he rode into the small town of Culpeper, VA, he was totally shocked by what he saw.

There in the middle of the town square was a minister tied to a whipping post, his back laid bloody and bare with the back bones of his ribs in view. This minister had been scourged mercilessly, like Jesus, with a metal laced whip.

"When they stopped beating him, I could see the bones of his rib cage. I turned to someone and asked what the man had done to deserve such a beating as this." — Patrick Henry.

The man being scourged was a man of the cloth who refused to accept a license. He was one of twelve who were locked in jail because they refused to accept a license. A license often means arbitrary control by a government that makes it a crime to do without a license what ordinarily would not be a crime. A License turns a Right into a Privilege.

Three days later they scourged him to death.

This was the incident which sparked Christian attorney Patrick Henry to write the famous words which later became the rallying cry of the Revolution.

"What is that Gentlemen's wish? What would they have? Is life so dear, or peace so sweet, as to be purchased at the price of slavery and chains? Forbid it Almighty God! I know not what course others may take, but as for me, Give me liberty or Give me death!"

Later he made this phrase part of his famous speech at St. John's Episcopal Church in Richmond, VA.

20
Jury Of Peers

Our forefathers felt that in order to have Justice, a "Jury of Peers" must be people who actually know the defendant. How else would they be able to judge motive and intent?

"Peers of the defendant" like the "Rights of the Jury" have been severely tarnished. It originally meant people who were "equals in station and rank" (Black's 1910), "free-holders of a neighborhood" (Bouvier's 1886), or "A companion; a fellow; an associate" (Webster's 1828).

Patrick Henry, and others, was deeply concerned about who has a right to sit on a Jury. Note our forefather's comments on the subject of "Peers."

"By the English Bill of Rights, a subject has a right to a trial by his peers. What is meant by his peers? Those who reside near him, his neighbors, and who are well acquainted with his character and situation in life." — Patrick Henry (The Debates in the Several State Conventions on the Adoption ofthe Federal Constitution (Elliot 3:579).

Originally, the Jury of Peers was designed as a protection for neighbors from outside oppression by the government.

"Why do we love this trial by jury? Because it prevents the hand of oppression from cutting you off ... This gives me comfort - that, as long as I have existence, my neighbors will protect me." — Patrick Henry (Elliot, 3:545, 546).

Mr. Holmes, from Massachusetts, argued strenuously that for Justice to prevail, the case must be heard in the vicinity where the fact was committed by a Jury of Peers.

"... a jury of the peers would, from their local situation, have an opportunity to form a judgment of the CHARACTER of the person charged with the crime, and also to judge the CREDABILITY of the witnesses." — Patrick Henry (Elliot 2:110).

"The people are the masters of both Congress and courts, not to overthrow the Constitution, but to over-throw the men who pervert it!" — Abraham Lincoln.

Mr. Wilson, signer of **"The unanimous Declaration,"** who also later became a Supreme Court Justice, stressed the importance of the Jurors knowing personally both the defendant and the witnesses.

"Where jurors can be acquainted with the characters of the parties and the witnesses — where the whole cause can be brought within their knowledge and their view — I know no mode of investigation equal to that of a trial by jury: they hear everything that is alleged; they not only hear the words, but they see and mark the features of the countenance; they can judge of

weight due to such testimony; and moreover, it is an inexpensive and expeditious manner of distributing justice. There is another advantage annexed to the trial by jury; the jurors may indeed return a mistaken or ill-founded verdict, but their errors cannot be systematical." — Elliot, 2:516.

"Those people who are not governed by GOD will be ruled by tyrants." — William Penn.

Edward Bushell and three fellow Jurors learned this lesson well. They refused to bow to the court. They believed in the absolute power of the Jury, although their eight companions cowered to the court.

The four Jurors spent nine weeks in prison, often without food or water, barely able to stand, and even threatened with fines, yet they would not give in to the judge.

Edward Bushell said, *"My liberty is not for sale,"* although he had great wealth and commanded an international shipping enterprise.

These "bumble heads" — so the court thought — proved that the power of the people was stronger than any power of government. They emerged total victors.

The year was 1670, and the case **Edward Bushell** sat on, as a Juror, was that of **William Penn**, who was on trial for violation of the **"Conventicle Act."** An elaborate Act which made the **Church of England** the only legal church.

The Act was struck down by their **"Not Guilty"** vote.

Freedom of Religion was established and became part of the English Bill of Rights and later part of the First Amendment to the U. S. Constitution.

In addition, the **Right to Peaceful Assembly** was founded, **Freedom of Speech**, and **Habeas Corpus** (bring the accused before the court). The first such writ ever issued by the Court of Common Pleas was used to free **William Penn**. This trial gave birth later to the concept of **Freedom of the Press**.

Had **Bushell** and his colleagues yielded to the guilty verdict sought by the prosecutor and the judge, **William Penn** most likely would have been executed, as he clearly at that time broke English law.

There would have been no **Liberty Bell**, no **Independence Hall**, no **Philadelphia**, and no **Pennsylvania**, for young **William Penn**, the founder of Pennsylvania, and leader of the Quakers, was on trial for his life.

His alleged crime was preaching and teaching a different view of the Bible than that of the Church of England. This appears innocent today, but at that time one could be **put to death** for such actions.

William Penn believed in freedom of religion, freedom of speech and the right to peaceful assembly. He had transgressed the government's law, but he had injured no one in doing so.

Those four heroic Jurors knew that only when actual injury to someone's person or property takes place is there a real crime. **No law is broken when no injury can be shown. There can be no loss, or termination of rights, unless actual damage is proven.**

Many imposter laws were repealed as a result of this case.

This trial made such an impact that every colony except

one, established the Jury as the *first liberty to maintain all other liberties.*

It was felt that the people's liberties could never be wholly lost as long as the Jury remained independent and strong, and that unjust statutes and laws could not stand when confronted by conscientious Jurors.

Jurors today face an avalanche of impostor laws.

Jurors not only have **the power and the right, but also the duty** to nullify bad laws by voting "Not Guilty".

At first glance, it would appear almost unfair — the power Jurors have over government — but essential, considering the historical track record of oppression that governments have wielded over private citizens.

Policy, Procedures & Protocols

21
Jefferson's Warnings

In 1789 Thomas Jefferson warned that the Judiciary, if given too much power, would ruin our Republic and destroy our Rights.

"The new Constitution has secured individual rights in the Legislative and Executive departments: but not in the Judiciary. It should have established trials by the people themselves, that is to say, by juries."

"The Judiciary of the United States is the subtle corps of miners constantly working under ground to undermine the foundations of our confederated fabric."

"The Federal Judiciary; an irresponsible body (for impeachment is scarcely a scarecrow), working like gravity by night and by day, gaining a little today and a little to- morrow, and advancing its noiseless step like a thief, over the field of jurisdiction, until all shall be usurped from the States, and the government of all be consolidated into one. . . . when all government in little as in great things, shall be drawn to Washington as the centre of all power, it will render powerless the checks provided of one government on another and will become as venal and oppressive as the government from which we separated."

"The opinion which gives to the judges the right to decide what laws are constitutional and what are not, not only for themselves in their own sphere of action, but for the legislative and executive also in their spheres, would make the judiciary a despotic branch."

"Judges should be withdrawn from the bench whose erroneous biases are leading us to dissolution. It may, indeed, injure them in fame or fortune; but it saves the Republic ..."

Inscribed on our hallowed **LIBERTY BELL** are these words:

"PROCLAIM LIBERTY THROUGHOUT ALL THE LAND UNTO ALL THE INHABITANTS THEREOF." — *Leviticus 25:10.*

"Government is not reason; it is not eloquence; it is force! Like fire, it is a dangerous servant and a fearful master." — George Washington.

"Woe to those who decree unjust statutes and to those who continually, record unjust decisions, to deprive the, needy of justice and to rob the poor of my people of their rights..." — Isaiah 10:1,2.

"My people are destroyed because of the lack of knowledge...!" — Hosea 4:6.

"The only thing necessary for evil to triumph is for

good m3en to do nothing." — Edmund Burke 1729-1797.

"If My people which are called by My name, shall humble themselves, and pray, and seek My face, and turn from their wicked ways; then will I hear from Heaven, and will forgive their sin, and will heal their land." — II Chron. 7:14.

"We must obey GOD rather than men." — Acts 5:29.

Policy, Procedures & Protocols

State Acknowledgment and Affirmation of Union, *circa 2011.*

Policy, Procedures & Protocols

State Acknowledgment and Affirmation of Union, *circa 2011.*

We the People of Maine Republic, a free and independent state, establish and continue a republican form of governance guaranteed by United States Constitution *circa 1789* and Bill of Rights *circa 1791;* and

We the People of Maine Republic hereby acknowledge and affirm that we are in union America; and by manifest will and mutual agreement of We the People on this free and independent state, we enjoy and lawfully protect our God given unalienable rights of life, liberty, and the pursuit of happiness; and

We the People of Maine Republic uphold constitutional laws, lawful treaties and lawful contracts; and enforcement thereof for this free and independent state and union for Republic for the united States of America; and

We the People hold that all officials, elected or appointed, for Republic for the united states of America, agree to protect the God given unalienable rights endowed to the people and to honor and protect the freedom and independence of states in union at all times in accord with Declaration of Independence *circa 1776,* Constitution *circa 1789,* bill of Rights *circa 1791,* and a republican form of governance, at all levels, shall be recognized, adhered to, and preserved.

This document was autographed on 20 Feb 2011 by:

The Chief Executive for the Legislative Branch;
The Chief Executive for the Executive Branch;
The Chief Executive for the Judicial Branch.

"My people are destroyed for a lack of knowledge." — Hosea 4:6.

Policy, Procedures & Protocols

"A wise man will hear, and will increase learning; and a man of understanding shall attain unto wise counsels."
— Proverbs 1:5.

Policy, Procedures & Protocols

"Trust in the Lord with all thine heart; and lean not unto thine own understanding.

In all thy ways acknowledge him, and he shall directs thy paths."
— Poverbs 3:5,6.

Republic for the united States of America
http://republicfortheunitedstates.org/

Bureau Of Republic Records
http://www.bureauofrepublicrecords.org

Manual for the united States Republic

An Introductory Review

Forming Jural Assemblies

Building Block Of The Republic

Other Publications

The Matrix As It Is: *A Different Point Of View*
http://tinyurl.com/6htky52

From Debt To Prosperity: *'Social Credit' Defined*
http://tinyurl.com/2vjgqay

Give Yourself Credit: *Money Doesn't Grow On Trees*
http://tinyurl.com/39eoywm

My Home Is My Castle: *Beware Of The Dog*
http://tinyurl.com/37wk48v

Commercial Redemption: *The Hidden Truth*
http://tinyurl.com/37tdbrf

Hardcore Redemption-In-Law: *Commercial Freedom And Release*
http://tinyurl.com/2ul4t5e

Oil Beneath Our Feet: *America's Energy Non-Crisis*
http://tinyurl.com/34dhbur

Untold History Of America: *Let The Truth Be Told*
http://tinyurl.com/36tkc9q

New Beginning Study Course: *Connect The Dots And See*
http://tinyurl.com/37n8cyj

Monitions of a Mountain Man: *Manna, Money, & Me*
http://tinyurl.com/377l66n

Maine Street Miracle: *Saving Yourself And America*
http://tinyurl.com/38lk966

Reclaim Your Sovereignty: *Take Back Your Christian Name*
http://tinyurl.com/392kzqr

Epistle to the Americans I: *What you don't know about The Income Tax*
http://tinyurl.com/3yz8mun

Epistle to the Americans II: *What you don't know about American History*
http://tinyurl.com/33cawzr

Epistle to the Americans III: *What you don't know about Money*
http://tinyurl.com/3az8r7w

www.ingramcontent.com/pod-product-compliance
Lightning Source LLC
Chambersburg PA
CBHW071326310526
45789CB00016B/923